The Extraordinary Life Of An Ordinary Housewife

A Memoir of Awakening, Healing Trauma, and Choosing to Live a Sacred Life

Heather Debreceni

Heather Debreceni Enterprises LLC

Dedication

With deepest reverence and boundless gratitude,
this book is lovingly dedicated to my beloved Guruji, Paramahamsa Prajnanananda,
to his Gurudev, Paramahamsa Hariharananda,
and to the sacred lineage of masters, saints, and sages of Kriya Yoga.
On my knees, I bow with humility, devotion and gratitude
for your presence in my life - for your unwavering guidance, your protection, your teachings,
and the quiet, powerful current of your healing grace.
Thank you for your gentle nudges when I wander from the path,
and for your boundless compassion and forgiveness when I falter.
It is through your grace that this path continues to unfold,
and through that same grace that is the quiet foundation beneath every
word written here.

Invocation Prayer

May these words meet you exactly where you are.

May they offer you moments of stillness

within the noise,

clarity within the uncertainty,

and connection within the spaces that feel separate.

May you remember, again and again,

that you are not alone on this path.

May you feel the quiet presence of guidance,

the steady support beneath your steps,

and the gentle unfolding of your own inner knowing.

May you move through these pages

with an open heart,

THE EXTRAORDINARY LIFE OF AN ORDINARY...

a softened mind,

and a willingness to simply allow.

And may you come home—

not to something outside of you,

but to the truth that has always lived within.

Aum. Amen

Contents

Foreword

BY SWAMI ATMAVIDYANANDA GIRI

There are books that entertain, books that inform, and books that pass through our hands like a gentle breeze. And then there are books like this one—books that arrive as a companion on the soul's journey, quietly placing a hand on your shoulder and saying, *"You are not alone. Your story matters. Your healing is possible."*

Heather's memoir is not the tale of someone who set out to be remarkable. It is the story of someone who set out simply to survive—and in doing so, discovered the extraordinary within herself. She writes not as a heroine sculpted by myth, but as a woman shaped by the raw, unfiltered textures of real life: trauma, silence, resilience, awakening, and the slow, courageous choice to live with intention and sacredness.

What makes this book powerful is not just what happened to her, but how she learned to meet her life with honesty and tenderness. Heather does not offer a polished narrative of triumph. She offers something far more valuable: the truth of a woman who learned to listen to her own inner voice after years of being taught to silence it. The truth of a mother who found healing not in perfection, but in presence. The truth of a human being who realized that the sacred is not found in distant temples, but in the kitchen, the laundry room, the quiet moments before dawn, and the trembling decision to choose herself.

This memoir is an invitation—to remember that awakening is not reserved for monks, mystics, or those who retreat from the world. It can unfold in the heart of a housewife standing at her sink, in the middle of a marriage, in the aftermath of pain, or in the stillness that follows a long-buried truth finally spoken aloud.

Heather's journey reminds us that the sacred life is not something we stumble upon. It is something we choose, again and again, with trembling hands and an open heart.

May this book be a lantern for anyone who has ever felt ordinary, unseen, or unsure of their own worth. May it remind you that your story, too, is extraordinary. And may it give you the courage to step into your own sacred life—one breath, one truth, one act of love at a time.

Swami Atmavidyananda Giri

Preface

WELCOME NOTE TO THE READER & READER'S ORIENTATION

Welcome Reader,

This book began as a conversation.

It grew out of many hours of reflection, storytelling, and shared inquiry between two women exploring the relationship between trauma, healing, faith, and the human body. What you will find in these pages is not a prescription or a universal roadmap. It is the lived experience of one woman's journey back to breath, back to her body, and ultimately back to God.

Along the way, the story touches on spiritual traditions, healing practices, and personal revelations that shaped that journey. These reflections are offered with humility and care, in the hope that they may illuminate something within your own experience. Every path of healing is deeply personal. What unfolds in these pages is simply one story of how that path revealed itself to one woman.

If you are holding this book, you may already be navigating your own questions about faith, illness, trauma, or transformation. Our hope is that these words meet you gently where you are and perhaps remind you that the path home—to your body, your spirit, and the Divine—often begins with listening.

Sacred Practices, Intention, and Responsibility

Before entering the stories and practices described in this book, it is important to express something clearly.

Some of the practices referenced here, such as soul retrieval, Life Between Lives work, Past Life Regression therapy, and other shamanic modalities, are considered sacred traditions within the cultures and lineages from which they come. These practices developed historically as tools for healing trauma, restoring balance, and addressing deep fractures within the soul.

They are not meant to be approached casually, commercially, or out of curiosity alone. When sacred tools are reduced to novelty or entertainment, their meaning can be distorted and harm can occur.

Intention matters. A practice entered with reverence, humility, and a genuine desire for healing is fundamentally different from one entered lightly. These are not experiences to "try," but processes that deserve respect and care.

Discernment in choosing practitioners is equally important. Anyone granted access to another person's emotional, energetic, or spiritual experience carries responsibility. Even well-meaning guides can cause harm if they lack the training required to support integration and safety.

This book does not invite imitation. It invites understanding.

THE EXTRAORDINARY LIFE OF AN ORDINARY...

If you feel drawn to explore any of the practices described here, seek trained and ethical practitioners, and remember that healing is not something to rush, prove, or perform. It unfolds in its own time.

Prologue

RADICAL SELFISHNESS: THE ROAD HOME TO GOD

Sometimes the body speaks the truth long before the mind is ready to hear it.

I was forty-seven years old when my body finally said what my soul had been whispering for decades: *We can't go on like this.*

I remember standing in my kitchen, one hand braced against the counter, trying to catch my breath after walking only a few steps across the room. My lungs burned. My chest felt tight. And a quiet, terrifying realization began to settle in: This wasn't temporary anymore.

By then, I carried a laundry list of diagnoses: eosinophilic asthma, eosinophilic esophagitis, suspected but unconfirmed mast cell activation syndrome, oral allergy syndrome, food and environmental anaphylaxis, and dyspnea so severe that every step felt like wading through wet cement. I was unstable on my feet, short of breath, and quietly reckoning with the fact that the survival outlook for my conditions was not encouraging.

My days revolved around medications: prednisone, Breo Ellipta, nebulizer treatments four times a day, Flonase, Zyrtec, famotidine, Dupixent, Asmanex, Montelukast, and more. My doctors told me I was "maxed out" on treatment. Beyond that, their suggestions were vague and halfhearted.

"Maybe walk on a treadmill," they said, as if my lungs and I hadn't already tried to bargain with gravity just to get from the bed to the bathroom.

It may or may not be important to mention, but I've never been a smoker. In my eyes, I was just a somewhat young grandmother, mother, wife, ordained minister, and retired Deputy Sheriff who also ran a successful divorce coaching practice. And above all, now, I was a woman who could not reliably trust her own breath.

This book is the story of how I came to understand that my body wasn't betraying me. It was telling me the truth.

It was telling the truth about the trauma I had carefully learned to minimize and organize my life around. It was telling the truth about a lifetime of giving from an empty cup, of confusing martyrdom for love, and of putting everyone else's needs before my own and calling it "service" or "devotion." It was telling the truth about how disconnected I had become from the living, breathing presence of God.

Not the God of dogma or fear or spiritual performance. The God of love. The God I had known as a child. The God I would later meet again on the breath.

When you are staring your own mortality in the face, life gets very simple, very quickly.

I wish I could tell you that I met that moment with unwavering faith and unshakable peace. The truth is, I was terrified. Not to mention, exhausted physically, emotionally, and spiritually. And quietly, I was heartbroken by how small my life had become, circumscribed by inhalers, lab results, and emergency plans. Was this really all it was going to be?

Therapy was one of the first doors I walked through, and I say this without hesitation: If you are living with chronic illness, profound stress, or unresolved trauma, a skilled therapist can be a godsend. The work I did there helped me begin to reframe my relationship with my body—from seeing it as an enemy to seeing it as a messenger.

Not long after a family vacation, where I smiled through photos and wheezed through nights, I made the decision to step away from social media. I felt a deep pull to go inward, away from the noise, the performance, and the subtle pressure to keep up appearances.

I made a quiet, radical decision: I would devote myself fully. To my faith, to inner peace, to whatever time I had left, and to the quality of that time.

It was during that season of retreat that I stumbled upon a book called *Breath: The New Science of a Lost Art* by James Nestor, which I will discuss more later in this book. At a time when every inhale felt like a negotiation, a book about breathing practically glowed from my Amazon recommended reading list.

Up until that moment, most of my "goals" had really been survival strategies dressed up as plans.

Lose weight.

Be more productive.

Push through.

Give more.

Do better.

Be better.

But when you're acutely aware that your time here is finite, "lose ten pounds" loses its shine.

I realized that what I needed wasn't more goals. I needed intentions—soul-level commitments that honored the preciousness of each breath.

I began with three:

1. Face my mortality with grace.

Not in surrender to death, but in acceptance of reality. I wanted to wake each day with gratitude, knowing that every sunrise was a gift, not a guarantee.

2. Live as long as possible, without fear.

I did not want to die. I still don't. I wanted to be here for my family, my calling, and my own unbecoming. I needed to stop treating my body as an afterthought and start honoring it as sacred.

3. Remember that every action, or inaction, matters.

Every choice was either a step toward or away from a longer, healthier, more aligned life. What I ate. How much water I drank. The way I spoke to myself. The invitations I accepted or declined. Every "yes" and every "no" carried weight.

As I began to track my pulse, oxygen levels, sleep, and weight through medical monitoring and my Fitbit, I watched something extraordinary happen: my inner shifts began to register in the data. It was as if my body had been waiting for me to choose it—to stand it on its side and to become its ally rather than its critic.

This is where the concept that would change my life and become a central pillar of this book was born: Radical Selfishness.

We are taught that giving is noble. And it is. But many of us, especially women, especially sensitive souls, and especially those drawn to healing and spiritual service, learn a version of giving that is quietly destructive.

We give from an empty cup.

We equate exhaustion with worth.

We confuse self-abandonment with love.

My body began to fail, in part, because I had become exquisitely skilled at abandoning myself. I wasn't prioritizing rest. I wasn't asking for help. I wasn't allowing myself to receive. I was saying yes when my entire being was begging me to say no.

Radical selfishness, as I eventually came to understand it, was not selfishness in the way the world uses the word. It was a fierce, loving, unapologetic commitment to my own life force.

It was the recognition that this body, this breath, and this energy were divinely given—on loan from the Source that created me—and that I was responsible for stewarding them well.

Radical selfishness forced me to ask myself questions like:

Do I really need to do this?

Is it loving to say yes to this if it shortens my time on this planet?

Would someone who genuinely loves me want me to agree to this at the expense of my health?

These questions became the filter I ran everything through: social invitations, family expectations, even well-intentioned requests cloaked in urgency.

Learning to say no, calmly, clearly, and without apology, is one of the most spiritual practices I have ever undertaken.

Not saying no out of bitterness.

Not saying no out of resentment.

But saying no out of love.

Love for my own soul.

Love for my partner, my children, and my community.

Love for the people who wanted me alive, present, and joyful for the long haul.

Radical selfishness, as I live and teach it now, is not about hoarding your time or guarding your heart with barbed wire. It is about filling your cup so completely—with rest, spirit, joy, and truth—that what spills over is authentic generosity, not obligation.

It was radical selfishness that led me to Kriya Yoga and shamanism, and it was radical selfishness that put me back on the path home to God.

When I signed up for my Kriya Yoga initiation weekend, I didn't know it would change my life. I only knew I was tired of being at war with my own breath.

What happened there was not a lightning bolt of mystical fireworks. It was quieter and far more profound.

I learned how to breathe. Truly breathe.

Kriya Yoga is more than movement or posture. It is a meditative technology of consciousness—a way of linking breath, body, mind, and soul so that your life force, your *prana*, begins to flow freely again. **Prana** (प्राण, prāṇa) is a Sanskrit term meaning "life force," "vital energy," or "breath of life."

As I committed to daily practice and deep meditation, I noticed tangible changes.

My morning peak flow numbers rose.

My resting pulse dropped.

My oxygen levels climbed from 95 percent to 99–100 percent.

For someone whose lungs had felt like hostile territory, these were not small improvements. They were miracles measured in data points.

More importantly, as my breath softened, my inner voice did too. I began to hear how cruel I had been to myself in the privacy of my own mind. I began to see how I had withheld from myself the very compassion I so freely offered to others.

Through Kriya, long hours in meditation, and the subtle, unmistakable presence of the Divine moving in my chest with every inhale, I started to practice something that always felt out of reach: self-compassion. Not self-pity. Not self-indulgence.

Self-compassion.

The kind of gentle, patient, unwavering kindness I imagined God extending to me, no matter how scared, messy, or imperfect I was. I slowly began to extend that same kindness to myself.

As my practice deepened, Kriya became a doorway into other realms of spiritual exploration.

Suddenly, a lifetime of multifaith study—biblical scholarship, mysticism, Wicca, Reiki, metaphysics, and even quantum physics—converged in a way that felt coherent. Instead of competing, all these paths began to braid together like a sacred cord. It was during this season that I felt an undeniable call toward shamanism.

Shamanism is an ancient, earth-honoring spiritual practice, often considered among the oldest in the world, in which a practitioner (shaman) enters altered states of consciousness to interact with spiritual realms for guidance, healing, and wisdom.

When I first encountered shamanism, I didn't think of it in those terms. I only knew that even without understanding all of its meaning, something in me recognized it immediately.

When I started reading the accounts of shamanic practitioners from different cultures, one theme struck me over and over: many of them had been called to their path through illness, crisis, or near-death experiences. They had been broken open, often against their will, and had learned to heal from the inside out. Their stories resonated in my bones. You'll learn more about this later in the book.

I enrolled in a formal shamanic training program and began working with a seasoned practitioner. Through that work, I learned to reconnect with the natural world, not as scenery or a backdrop, but as a living, sentient community of allies and teachers. The trees, the wind, the stones, the animals, the ancestors... all became part of a vast, loving web that I had been too busy, too sick, or too afraid to fully feel.

Shamanism did not replace my Christian roots or my Wiccan priestess-hood; it expanded them. It invited me into a direct relationship with Spirit, unmediated by doctrine or fear. Miraculously, Kriya Yoga and shamanism also brought me back to Jesus, not as a distant authority, but as a healer, a mystic, and a brother in suffering and resurrection.

The God I met in this integration—through Kriya breaths, shamanic journeys, Reiki channels, crystal grids, scripture, myth, mantra, and simple silence—was not a God offended by my questions or my multiplicity.

This God was spacious.

This God was kind.

This God was present in my lungs, in my cells, and in the very illnesses that had once felt like a curse.

Today, as I write these words, just a few short months before my fiftieth birthday, my life looks very different from the life of the woman who could barely cross a room without gasping.

I no longer rely on nebulizer treatments four times a day.

I've stopped using a secondary steroid inhaler (though I keep it close, just in case).

With my doctor's guidance, I've reintroduced some foods that were once unthinkable.

My oxygen levels stay at 99–100 percent.

My resting pulse hovers around 50.

My blood pressure is a healthy 120/65.

My lungs test like those of someone a decade younger.

My heart scans strong and clear.

THE EXTRAORDINARY LIFE OF AN ORDINARY...

I drink water like it's holy (because it is). I eat vegetables with almost every meal. I've let go of sugar, as well as any added salt to my food. I choose decaf most days. Some weight has fallen away, not through punishment or dieting, but through devotion to balance, wellness, and intentional living.

I still work closely with my medical team. I still live in a human body with a history of illness and trauma.

This is not a fairy tale. It is a testimony.

The turning point was not any single tool, though Kriya Yoga, shamanism, Reiki, crystals, medicine, and conventional therapy have each played their part.

What was the turning point?

I chose devotion.

I chose my life.

I chose my breath.

I chose to stop abandoning myself in the name of love, service, or spirituality.

I chose radical selfishness as a doorway to radical love.

This book was born from that choice. It is part memoir, part guidebook, and part love letter. Yes, love letter.

Love letter to...

...anyone who has been told that their pain is "all in their head."

...anyone whose faith has been weaponized against them.

...anyone who has given and given, until they are too sick to keep giving and are secretly afraid it might already be too late.

In these pages, I will share how trauma—sometimes obvious, sometimes subtle—pulled me away from my connections with God, my own soul, and my body. I will do my best to show you how that disconnect manifested as illness, burnout, and quiet despair.

Then I will walk you through some of the practices, choices, and perspectives that helped me find my way home.

We will talk about breath and belief, science and spirit, and setting both boundaries and intentions.

We will explore what it means to reclaim your body as sacred ground, to honor your nervous system as an oracle, and to trust your intuition as a legitimate form of guidance.

Most of all, we will practice together what I am still practicing every day:

Extending deep compassion to ourselves.

Listening to our bodies as messengers, not enemies.

Claiming the courage to be "radically selfish" in service of a larger love.

If you are holding this book, you are likely already on a journey of healing, awakening, or return. You may be tired. You may be scared. You may be hopeful in that fragile, tentative way that feels like reaching out in the dark for a hand you're not entirely sure is there.

Let this prologue be my way of placing my hand in yours and saying:

You are not alone.

Your body is not your enemy.

Your longing for God, for peace, for wholeness, and for breath is holy.

There is a path forward. It may not look the way you expected, but it is here, now, under your feet.

This is the story of how I found my own path forward.

With love and humility,
Heather

Introduction

THE CALL TO SPEAK

For as long as I can remember, my throat has felt heavy. When I laughed, even when I "easily" spoke in public, there was a hidden part of me holding back. Words pressed against my ribs like birds against a cage.

On the surface I was "together," but inside I lived with old fears: If I tell the truth, I'll be punished. If I show myself, I'll be burned. Those fears weren't just metaphors. They were cellular, memory impressions of other lifetimes where speaking openly got me exiled, tortured, or silenced.

In spiritual language, they call it the "witch wound." In practical terms, it meant I'd learned to hide—to modulate my voice and to speak in ways that felt safe but not true.

Now, I recognize I've carried a lot of blockage in my throat chakra. Not just from this lifetime, but as a residue carried across many—fear around speaking my truth because of persecution.

That memory lived in my body as if it had just happened. It's why the nudge to speak out, even in something as simple as a Facebook Live, felt so terrifying, yet so necessary.

Nine months before this book began, the whisper to tell my story on a bigger platform became a shove. In meditation one morning, I heard it clearly: *Do the Facebook Lives again.* It sounded ridiculous. *Why Facebook? Why now?* Due to my health issues, I had purposely given up hosting regular Facebook Lives about business, social media, and other random real and raw topics. But the nudge was insistent.

The next day, I sat in my backyard with my plate of olives and pumpkin seeds in one hand and nerves buzzing. *Ok, I guess we're doing this live video thing again.* I pressed that "Go Live" button and braced myself.

Only this time, it wasn't just me talking. Words came through me, not from me.

A clarity and confidence I didn't recognize poured out. My body relaxed even as my heart raced. When I stopped, I stared at the screen, blinking. People weren't just scrolling by; they watched, they listened, and they commented. Something in them recognized a very real, raw truth when they heard my words. As if they were seeing themselves in me.

I trusted what was coming through me, but I needed to know I wasn't imagining these feelings.

Around the same time, I booked my first Akashic Records reading. I wanted confirmation I wasn't imagining these feelings.

Akashic Records are a comprehensive, energetic log of all human and universal events (past, present, and potential future). They are often described as a cosmic database or vibrational history accessed through meditation, prayer, or specific intentional keys and used for personal growth, healing, and understanding the soul's path. My intuitive life coach and mentor at the time knew of a person who could offer Akashic Records readings. Through her recommendation, I booked the session without speaking with the practitioner beforehand.

The Akashic Records reader didn't sugarcoat it: "Stop questioning. You already know. Surrender to the process."

I laughed out loud because the advice sounded exactly like my soul: detached, slightly exasperated, but deeply loving. This feeling, this knowing was so familiar, I often felt as if my soul was saying it in a mildly inconvenienced tone: *Why are you asking this again? You already know the answer. Stop questioning and surrender.*

That reading continued to go deeper. She went on to tell me to let go of all relationships that weren't serving me. At the time, I felt she was pointing toward my marriage. I really don't have many outside relationships, and my marriage was struggling. More importantly, at the time, I wasn't ready to hear this.

Here's the thing about psychic guidance: sometimes it feels like pure healing, and other times, it's like a jolt of truth you wish you could unhear. And sometimes, the information isn't delivered in a healing way; it's delivered in a way that dysregulates your entire body.

I learned then how important spiritual boundaries are. Even with the most well-meaning guides, healers, and mentors, you must set boundaries for yourself. It's important you know how to discern what you're ready to act on and what you're not. It's incredibly important that your practitioners know how to properly deliver the message as part of *your healing story*. Their role should be to help you integrate the information and messages experienced into your life and your healing.

In my hopes of both understanding the last reading and escaping the whole "surrender to telling your story" message, a few days later I booked a reading with a different Akashic Records practitioner, Alissa Williams with Sapphire Soul Wellness. I wasn't trying to undo what I'd heard . . . I was trying to understand how to live with it.

This time, the reader didn't know anything about me; we'd never met through any other means before this session. This anonymity also reassured my analytical mind that the information I was going to receive was unbiased.

Lo and behold, this new reader barely glanced at me before saying: "Why are you here? You've already gotten that answer. Yes, you need to tell, but more specifically, write your story."

"But I'm already telling my story and doing those Facebook Lives," I protested.

She shook her head. "No. Not just Social Media videos. A book. You're being called to write a book."

Her words landed like a punch in my gut. *A book? Me?*

The final push came during a Vanaprastha Retreat I was attending in Chicago. When teaching about ways we could contribute our wisdom to the community, Swami Atmavidyananda Giri mentioned that we could write a book and share our experiences as a means of giving back to the community and sharing our knowledge. It was the final blow to my resistance; it was another breadcrumb I needed to follow.

You might be asking, "What was the problem? Why not just start writing?"

The problem was as simple and as complex as our trauma. It started with the things my mind has been telling me for years. Things like, *I can't write.* I just wasn't born with that "writing gene." When I tried to write my story in the past, it ended up sounding like an instruction manual got crossed with a police report. How would this be different?

Or was this one of those "stories" we tell ourselves? Maybe. But I also thought about my health. It was so fragile, and my energy was so limited. Writing felt impossible. But now two strangers and a swami who I highly respected had echoed the same message: "You must tell your story. In written form."

Was this just ego talking? Who am I to share my story? Who am I to be considered a guide? I continued to sit with it.

One of my meditation practices is to expand my heart and crown chakras until I feel myself become vast. This practice helps me live energetically expanded, open, and vulnerable.

During one of my meditations, expanding the heart and crown chakras as wide as they could go, a different knowing came through: *This isn't about ego. It's your assignment. Your soul chose this. You're being asked to be a guiding light: a soul healer.*

That day's practice gave me a glimpse of what it meant to carry this assignment with reverence instead of fear. There was no hiding from it this time. I had spent so long trying to bypass my own pain that therapy, medication, exercise, and even meditation had been used as a numbing agent.

The message kept coming back:

There's no bypassing.

Speak.

Share.

THE EXTRAORDINARY LIFE OF AN ORDINARY...

Show the cracks.

Tell your story.

What was I to do? I was committed to this path: to healing, to reconnection, and to devotion. I no longer felt like it was a choice. So I began "telling" my story. First, with the live videos via social media.

One live video after another. Words I didn't plan poured through, naturally and with conviction. There were times I didn't even know everything I said until afterwards. People started writing comments like, "You're putting words to what I've felt for years."

It terrified me and thrilled me. It was the first taste of what would become this book. The call was no longer a whisper. It was a command. As the command demanded the story be told, a collaboration was born.

I needed a soul that I trusted and could be deeply vulnerable with to help me get the story out. As we delve into how this Ordinary Housewife starts living an Extraordinary Life, you'll occasionally encounter reflections from my writer, collaborator and sister of the soul, Gina, who is a witness to this process.

CHAPTER ONE

The Messenger

THE BODY AND HOW SHE KEPT SCORE

My body has always been my messenger. For years I treated it like a stubborn, unloved child, abusing it, forcing it to comply, ignoring its cries, and silencing its whispers. I could outrun my exhaustion with sheer willpower, medicate my pain away, and distract myself with work or caretaking. But the body doesn't forget. It knows how to keep score when the soul's wounds go unheeded.

From the outside, I looked strong, tough even. A big part of me not only thrived in that image, but at the time, it needed it. As a true Gemini, I guess I assimilated the Gemini twin who carried the stronger, masculine, warrior side—Pollux. He was my ticket to life for a long time. Search and rescue, private security, law enforcement, the academy, and even the daily posture of survival—they all sharpened that edge.

But another side got buried, bullied even. My intuitive, softer, feminine side was completely obscured in the process. I learned to listen to command structures, push past limits, deny rest, and then some.

Who paid the price?

The messenger: my body.

At first, I ignored the whispers in the smallest ways. I drank less water so I wouldn't have to take breaks. Yep, I saw bathroom urges as interruptions rather than signals. I brushed off asthma symptoms because I could just push through, or so I thought. I ate foods that I knew didn't agree with my body because they were convenient and didn't require time away from all my responsibilities.

A friend once told me, "Just ask your lungs what's wrong." At the time I thought, *What does that even mean?* Later I discovered through meditation that my body was always speaking; I just had to listen.

This story isn't just about me or my survival; it's meant to serve as another messenger. This is about your survival too. You picked up this book for a reason. If you're still learning how to listen to your messenger, let my story help. You just have to listen.

In 2018, the collapse came suddenly. One moment I was managing my asthma, the next I was fighting for my life. During my fifth or sixth allergy immunotherapy shot, my body went into full-blown anaphylaxis. I was rushed to the ICU, where I stayed for six days.

At one point, I was in one-on-one care because my cardiac function had become unstable from repeated doses of epinephrine and the effects of anaphylaxis. They pumped me full of prednisone, IV Benadryl, and the strongest COPD inhaler on the market. I remember lying there, monitors beeping, my chest battling for air while my mind still screamed, *Just push harder, you can get through this.*

Except, there are places willpower just won't do!

My body was done carrying the weight of my denial. I nearly left my children and my husband. I almost didn't live to see my daughter get married or to meet my grandbaby. What a gift I would've missed.

Looking back, I can see that my body had been warning me all along; I just hadn't listened. Even after that crisis, I still resisted. I went back to pushing, back to caretaking, and back to silencing. But the messages kept coming. The body will whisper until it screams.

In 2023, the second explosion came not from biological disease (although it manifested as such) but from my own home. A betrayal that pierced what little safety I had left. While I was struggling with my health, my husband was fighting his own inner battles. Those battles led him to make choices that didn't only impact him but also the foundation of how I viewed our relationship and my role in it. This discovery sent me spiraling into the worst medical flare of my life.

My asthma ramped into chaos. Finally, in mid 2024, after over nine months of fighting for every breath, doctors finally diagnosed me with MCAS and dyspnea: oxygen deprivation, dizziness, and a warning of 51 percent mortality. My nervous system collapsed into pure rage.

Pure rage is the only way I can describe how I felt. I told myself, "Burn it all, all of it." I literally wanted to burn my whole life to the ground. At that moment, I felt like it was all a lie and meant nothing.

I was angry, and now, I'm so grateful for that anger. That was the moment I realized I needed help. The betrayal, the flares, and the fury were destroying me from the inside out. This was the moment that sent me into a different kind of spiral. I was going to tend to Heather: to her body, her mind, her heart, and most importantly, her SOUL. Throughout my life, I was no stranger to traditional therapy. It was an anchor I knew to go to, and it's still one I recommend. This time, it wasn't necessarily something I wanted to do, but my body was giving me no choice. It was speaking what my mouth could not say: *You are not safe. You are not being true to yourself.*

Today, I see my body's intelligence. It was never betraying me; it was screaming on my behalf. Every flare, every collapse, and every racing heartbeat was my body saying: *Pay attention. This is not who you are. This is not what you came here to do.*

In my journal, during one of those desperate conversations with Spirit, spitting anger and rage, I asked: *Why?* The answer that came was simple: *Because it had to be dramatic, otherwise you wouldn't have listened.*

Here's that theme again: *Listen.*

If you're reading this and have been ignoring the body's whispers, my friend, this is your queue: *LISTEN.*

Back to those conversations with Spirit…

When I asked: *What is my purpose?*

The reply was clear: *You are a soul healer.*

When I asked: *Who am I?*

The voice said: *A divine being of light. The atom point and the infinite.* This conversation happened over and over again. Those words became anchors.

They gave me language for what my body had been trying to tell me all along. Those sacred words led me into shamanic work, where my first personal soul retrieval showed me the pieces of myself I had abandoned.

Soul retrieval is an ancient shamanic practice aimed at recovering, healing, and reintegrating fragmented parts of a person's vital essence (soul) lost due to trauma, shock, or emotional distress.

The hardest part of a healing journey isn't the illness itself. The hardest part is facing the truth; no bypass works. You can't therapy it away, exercise it away, or even meditate it away.

The only way out is through.

You have to be willing to feel through the grief, through the rage, and through the terror, and have the courage to let the body finally unclench.

The soul may be infinite, but the body is finite. It demands honesty. It demands presence. It demands that we keep score until we finally learn to read and interpret what it's trying to tell us.

Chapter Two

Progress Looks Like Chaos

For years I thought healing was supposed to look like a steady climb. You do the therapy, the spiritual practices, and the journaling, and eventually you arrive. Right?

Arrive at what? Peace? A clean, polished, whole, enlightened existence? That's the picture I carried, the lie I chased.

Buckle up buttercup, because the truth is, healing looks more like a big pile of chaos. It loops. It doubles back. It falls apart just when you think you've figured it out. Think of your healing journey like an infinity loop. The figure eight that never ends, circling the same wound from new directions each time.

Lean into the suck. Don't shy away from it. It's supposed to be chaotic. It's supposed to come back around until the wound is no longer attached to you (or you to it).

One of the spiritual teachers I have been blessed to learn from, gave me a metaphor I've carried ever since hearing it: "It is like holding up a filthy glass and slowly wiping it clean. At first the glass is cloudy. You can't see through it. But each pass of the rag clears another layer until, eventually, the glass gleams."

Healing doesn't mean you never touch the dirt again. Living life adds more dust and dirt to the glass. But each healing loop through the mess leaves you clearer than before. This pattern of looping showed up everywhere: in my body, my relationships, and my spirituality. Just when I thought I'd made progress, another wave of illness or betrayal or grief would knock me down. I hated it. I thought I was regressing. I thought wounds would never heal.

Over time I learned that those spirals weren't setbacks. They were the depth of healing.

The Dawn Of Growth

We refer to this time of year as the "dead of winter." We see the snow burying the grass. The bare trees and the leaves dry and brown on the ground.

We think that it is dead darkness underneath.

We wonder if it will ever grow back the same.

We face that same feeling in our lives when things are dark.

We feel buried, and we feel overwhelmed.

But like in nature, spring comes or the snow melts. You realize that it isn't the dead of winter. It's the dawn of growth.

You realize that underneath the surface, things are building their energy, they're growing new leaves, growing new buds.

The flowers are starting to bloom, and that is what life really is, even when it's dark.

Even when we're overwhelmed, spring comes and brings light. Snow melts and growth is revealed.

It is not the dead of winter; it's the dawn of growth.

-Heather Debreceni

January 19th, 2024

Sometimes I compare healing to the seasons. Winter looks like death, but underground, the soil is alive with preparation and reparation. Healing is like that. You think nothing is happening, but life is germinating in the dark. In fact, my current spiritual mentor helped me realize that some of my most difficult periods were not personal regressions at all, but tied to planetary and seasonal cycles. Recognizing that connection stopped me from turning natural rhythms into shame. We are much like nature; we are nature. We're supposed to go through changes, seasons, death, and renewal; it's all part of the loop.

Past Life Regression therapy gave me another lens. **Life Between Lives** (LBL) refers to the spiritual state or dimension a soul inhabits between incarnations, often accessed through deep hypnotic regression.

In one Life Between Lives session, I traveled back to the 1700s to a stark, lonely land in Wyoming. I was a woman, cold and dying alone in a barn after my family had perished. While I didn't die in that moment of the regression, the lesson from that point was solitude and learning how to be alone. At death, many years later in that lifetime, there was peace. The lesson was as follows: Even when life feels cold and alone in a moment, by learning from it, we can create growth, change, and peace for our futures.

When the practitioner asked me to re-enter the body after that death, my soul refused. It wanted to move forward, not back. She told me she had never seen this before. That memory from that lifetime carried a wound I had dragged into this life: a deep loneliness and an ache to belong. Seeing it and naming it softened its grip. My soul was ready to move on from this wound.

During another session, something extraordinary happened. While answering questions under hypnosis, my neck grew uncomfortable. I paused mid-sentence. Then I felt my soul send a message to my body to reposition my neck. It gently adjusted me with reverence, love, and care before the session could continue. The message was unmistakable: *My soul takes better care of this body than I do.*

At that moment, I realized this body was not a prison and not a punishment. It was an agreement. It was a blessing my soul had chosen knowingly, even with its limitations, because it could still carry out its purpose. This body was in fact part of why the soul picked this vessel. From there, everything started to shift in me. Every flare, every collapse, and every struggle was not betrayal; it was soul and body working together to guide me back to truth. My soul had been whispering all along: *I've got you. You're not alone in this body. I chose it with you, and I'll carry it with you.*

As my understanding deepened, so did my spiritual practice. I was drawn toward a type of surrender, renunciation. In the Hindu traditions, this phase of life is referred to as the Vanaprastha Ashram (life stage). It represents a gradual detachment from worldly duties to focus on spirituality. Not fully renouncing as a monk or nun, not necessarily through vows, but as a chosen devotion. A period of life where you transition from being the head of the household to the Elder in the community.

At the time, I didn't yet have language for what this path would become.

During a Kriya Yoga retreat in late April 2025, it was announced that for the first time in the United States, Kriya Yoga International would be offering a Vanaprastha program for a small and select group of applicants. This pre-monastic training was designed to support those entering—or already living within—the Vanaprastha Ashram of life and seeking guidance on how to proceed. I applied.

I was younger than the usual age range for the program, but to my surprise, I was accepted. This was my first really immersive program within the Kriya community. Twenty-one days of teachings, meditations, and living in the Ashram taught me so much about what it means to love myself, God, and others. I learned what it means to be compassionate while remaining detached from the ups and downs of life going on around me. It was both an incredibly humbling and exhilarating experience. It's where I made a more conscious decision to commit to this lifestyle. And it's also where I received confirmation that telling my story as a book was a soul level assignment.

Now, I walk a path of renunciation without formal vows.

I volunteer my time within both the Kriya community and the wider community in my area. I devote hours each day to meditation, and just as many to spiritual study. I do this while holding the possibility of taking full vows later—when I, my family, and my guru are aligned and ready for that transition.

Funny enough, what started out as a fiery decision to put myself first has transformed into a beautifully devoted life: a life built on putting service to others above self. I've come to realize that every experience had, every trauma, every skill mastered, and every lesson learned was never about or for me. It was always about and for God. Those lessons were learned to help others, maybe even you.

I have been blessed by God to learn how to listen and heal while transitioning my life and perspective.

This choice isn't about abandoning life or my obligations. It isn't a life that you rush into to escape your current life. It isn't a trendy lifestyle choice. It's a calling. It's about choosing to live with fewer distractions, closer to the silence where the soul speaks. It's about choosing a life of devotion with the pursuit of self-realization as the goal.

Healing doesn't erase the chaos. It just transforms how I hold it.

The infinity loop still carries me back to familiar wounds, but now I see the circling as polishing. Like wiping the glass clean again and again, until the soul's light shines through. Progress looks like chaos. Healing looks like collapse. And wholeness looks like allowing it all to be part of the path.

CHAPTER THREE

The Making of Me

When someone asks what your earliest memories are, some of us go to precious memories—childlike, playful, and adventurous. For some of us, the memories are not so precious. While my childhood wasn't all horrible, my earliest memories are of being told through actions that who I was wasn't enough.

As a little girl, I was quiet and shy, often clinging close to my mother's side. Before I had the words to express it, I often sensed that the world around me wasn't safe. At an early age, my instincts told me to stay close, observe, and hold tight. My instincts knew that adults around me weren't always safe. But instead of reassurance, I was teased.

My stepfather called me a "cling-on," and others made jokes about how I always hung on my mother's hip. More than once I was pushed away so the adults could talk, drink, and indulge in drugs without having to worry about having a child present.

The unspoken message was clear: You don't belong here; your feelings of fear and insecurity are a burden on others.

What I felt was real.

Instead of being taught how to honor that intuition, I learned to bury it. I forced myself to be more extroverted, more talkative, and more adaptable, even though my natural state was quiet, tender, and observant.

This was the beginning of the wounds, learning early that my feelings didn't matter and my intuition wasn't trustworthy. I split into two selves: the outward girl who could charm and adjust, and the inward child who still longed for safety and truth.

It didn't help that I looked different from much of my family. My darker skin, curly hair, and fuller features marked me as "other" in a household shaped by my stepdad's Irish Catholic identity. My stepfather teased me about it, making comparisons that cut deeply. I carried those looks in the mirror as proof that I didn't belong.

Later, when the DNA tests came back, I laughed at the hot mess of it all. Results from 23andMe and Ancestry confirmed what I'd always suspected: I was a swirl of Indigenous American, Portuguese, Spanish, German. And in an ironic twist, the largest portion of my genetic makeup turned out to be Irish and Scottish.

As for my Native American ancestry, my mother had long believed my biological father carried Blackfoot roots, though it was never fully confirmed. What did feel meaningful to me, through my own spiritual lens and the shamanic work I would later step into, was the pattern I began to notice across my ancestry. In different cultural forms, I saw traditions connected to healers, mystics, and those who walked between worlds.

I don't say that as a proclamation, but as a framework that helped me make sense of myself. The very features that once made me feel alien in childhood began to feel less like shame and more like context. Not proof of destiny, but a thread I chose to follow.

Even as a child, I felt that pull toward the sacred. At six years old, I told my stepfather I wanted to be a nun. He brushed me off and told me I couldn't be a nun because I wasn't born Catholic. But the longing was real. It wasn't about doctrine; it was about devotion. I would bow instinctively to priests and nuns when I saw them, honoring something I didn't yet have words for. That sense of reverence was in me from the start.

School brought another layer of wounding. I have severe dyslexia and didn't learn to read until third or fourth grade. Multiple teachers told me I was "stupid" and would never learn. Numbers flipped, words blurred, and I couldn't pronounce new ones no matter how hard I tried. Foreign languages felt nearly impossible. Even when I managed to succeed later in life, the voices of those early teachers echoed. My mom tried to soften them by saying I was "smart in a different way," but to me that still meant I wasn't enough. I spent years overcompensating, always trying to prove my intelligence to others and to myself.

And then there was the sexualization—too young, too fast—before I understood what it meant. Some of those unsafe adults were predators. Adults who saw my young body and innocence as prey, without thought to the soul that resided within. They were so disconnected from their souls that they couldn't honor mine.

That imbalance left scars that followed me into adulthood. I came to believe that my only worth in relationships was as a sexual being, not as a full soul.

The combination of wounds—being dismissed as too sensitive, marked as different, branded as stupid, and sexualized before I was ready—fractured my sense of self. I carried those cracks for decades, filling them with striving, perfectionism, and roles designed to make me acceptable.

But the soul always circles back.

Years later, when my granddaughter was born, I looked at her and wept. From the moment of her conception, my daughter and I had made a conscious choice to honor her soul. I spoke to her while she was still in the womb as though she were already whole. Now, watching her grow, I nurture her in ways I was never nurtured. I see her bow to a Buddha statue and recognize in her the same devotion I once longed to openly display. She will never be dismissed for her sensitivity and spiritual openness, not if I have anything to do with it.

Seeing my granddaughter exposed me to my own childhood. It gave me compassion for that quiet, shy little girl I once was. It reminded me that even in my deepest wounding, the sacredness never left me.

This is the making of me—not just the pain, but the persistence. The quiet child who clung close for safety. The young woman who longed for devotion. The adult who worked too hard to prove her worth. The grandmother who now recognizes her own innocence reflected in a child's eyes.

I was made from contradictions: dismissed but devoted, wounded but wise, scarred but sacred. And piece by piece, I am remembering that every part of me belongs.

CHAPTER FOUR

Breaking, Then Becoming

I was shaped early by a man who was both a teacher and a tyrant. My stepfather was protective, strong, and intelligent, but he was also volatile and controlling. I idolized his strength and loyalty, but I also absorbed his rigidity. His rules became my survival code: how to date, how to speak, when to come home, etc. He even decided when I should break up with a boyfriend if he thought the boy was a distraction. Love was conditional. Loyalty was demanded. As a teenager, I didn't know where his protection ended and his dysfunction began.

It took years to understand that he didn't follow his own rules, including not being loyal to my mom in the most fundamental way in their marriage, and yet he loved her deeply.

That set the stage for how I understood relationships. In my world, sex did not equal love. Sex was currency, a way to prove my value, a way to feel momentarily wanted. Love was something else: distant, elusive, and un-achievable. I was too young and too inexperienced to know the difference, and those early distortions became the blueprint for my choices.

A teen boyfriend became the first lesson in relationship violence. I was sixteen. He refused to hear "no," even when I was sick or struggling to breathe with asthma. Fights became physical, sometimes escalating to the point that I was genuinely unsafe. My parents eventually stepped in, pulled me out of school for a few days for my safety, and ended the relationship. I felt relief and shame in equal measure. Relief that someone had noticed I was in danger, shame that I couldn't protect myself. That relationship confirmed a story I carried for years: I wasn't worth real love, only control and conflict.

My career path unfolded in the same rhythm: breaking, then becoming. I started in search and rescue, then moved to private security, drawn to environments where survival and protection were currency. I told myself I was helping others, but deep down I was learning to protect myself under uniforms and authority. That path led me into corrections, a world that hardened me and, in its own way, saved me.

But before corrections, there was my first marriage to my children's bio-logical father. Meeting him seemed like stability, like safety. We met while both working in private security. Before we got married, I did what I was taught and overlooked my intuitive warnings. At the time, he represented something familiar: strong, silent, and protective. We got engaged. Shortly after, I became pregnant and hoped to build a family. We also got married quicker than expected. But what followed wasn't stability; it was survival.

The pattern of controlling behavior, absenteeism, and the inability to meet me in the depth I longed for continued to follow me in our marriage. The day our daughter was born, I looked at her in my arms, and instantly my focus shifted entirely to her. From my perspective, at the time, it felt as though my husband remained detached, while I was forever changed. Looking back on it now, I can intellectually understand that my perspective was very different from his reality. However, at that point, I wasn't in an emotional or healed space where I could view his behavior from a place of compassion.

Motherhood forced me to put food in my body when I would have otherwise controlled or starved it. I had battled anorexia and bulimia, using control of my body as a way to manage chaos. But pregnancy forced me to surrender to a larger purpose. For the first time, I saw my body as capable of creation, not just destruction.

As the situation at home became less stable, corrections became my lifeline. In that environment, I found community, a family of uniforms bonded by danger and routine. But this was also a place of soul loss; it was all around. We were taught that compassion wasn't part of the job. "If your agency wants you to have compassion," the old saying went, "they'll issue it to you."

Yet, I still had moments where my humanity broke through. My marriage was failing, but I needed to hold onto some sort of hope; I had children to raise. I remember restraining a mentally ill woman, the way her body struggled under my hands, and the way her eyes pleaded even when words failed. I remember watching inmates, some hardened, some broken, and feeling waves of empathy that I had to suppress just to get through the shift. Each time I buried that compassion, a piece of my soul went quiet.

It was there that I learned how easily survival can masquerade as belonging.

By the time I left my marriage, I had grown into strength through my career, through the paycheck I brought home, and through the realization that I didn't need approval to survive. But independence didn't come easy. It came with anger, with financial fear, and with the exhaustion of single parenting. There were nights when my daughter looked at me in uniform as

I stood over her yelling about chores or homework not done, and I realized with horror that she wasn't seeing her mother; she was staring at an armed authority figure who terrified her.

My first divorce and subsequent co-parenting weren't smooth sailing. Things we didn't agree on in marriage didn't disappear. We no longer had to play nicely with one another. The gloves came off, and nobody was winning, especially not our children.

That realization pushed me into therapy. My therapist asked me, "How would you talk to him if he were an inmate?" It was a jarring question, but it changed everything. It gave me a framework to manage my communication—with my ex-husband, with my children, and with myself. Instead of erupting, I learned how to pause and to use the same boundaries and professionalism I carried at work inside my home.

Therapy also taught me that my reality wasn't the only one that mattered. It became clear early on that our son experienced the world differently. If I wanted a real relationship with him, I had to learn how to meet him where he was, not where I expected him to be.

Spending time in his world changed me. It showed me that what we call "reality" is deeply shaped by perception. Each of us builds our understanding of the world based on how we interpret the people, experiences, and environments around us.

Life moves forward and cycles repeat.

My second marriage followed another cycle of hope and betrayal. Infidelity reopened old wounds. This time, however, I wasn't the same woman that I was in my first marriage. I had begun studying the Bible, sitting in therapy, and seeking tools instead of distractions. I learned about attraction and about how the men who looked like protectors—the "bad boys," often with tattoos—were really mirrors of my unhealed "father" wound.

In a moment of clarity after my second divorce, I sat at the table with a pile of bills and realized no one was coming to rescue me. That was the moment something in me finally grew up. It was terrifying and liberating all at once. I would rescue myself. But what I know now is that *God* rescued me by showing me the path forward through these cycles.

And slowly, with work and dedication, I not only pulled myself up, but I was learning to listen when God whispered.

I moved into a tiny apartment in North Fort Myers, Florida, started managing money on my own, and found ways to support my children. I took my kids to the beach, to the movies, and to all the places I once thought you only went with a partner—as a *family*. I began to enjoy my own company, to feel the faint glimmer of freedom in solitude. Every ending, every betrayal, and every broken relationship had stripped me down. It was in the stripping that I was becoming.

Breaking taught me boundaries. Becoming taught me resilience. The path was never neat. It was messy, angry, sometimes shame-filled, and often lonely. But each break cracked me open to the becoming that followed.

This is the rhythm of my life: breaking and becoming, again and again. At the end of each cycle, a little more of my soul revealed its strength, and the woman who emerged was closer to the one I was meant to grow into.

CHAPTER FIVE

When the Soul Goes Quiet

What I Mean by "Soul"

When people ask me what it means to be disconnected from the soul, I usually feel the need to start by explaining how I understand the soul in the first place. It isn't an abstract or poetic idea—it's something you experience. I've brushed up against mine in meditation, in stillness, and in those moments when the inner noise quiets just enough for something deeper to surface.

The soul is pure. Not "good" in a moral sense, not naïve or saintly—just pure. Neutral. Kind. Loving without condition or expectation. It's like the emotional equivalent of a newborn fawn: gentle, unguarded, and without malice or agenda. Present.

When I think of true love, the kind that isn't possessive, jealous, or driven by fear, that's the soul. You see that same quality in beings like Jesus or the great masters across traditions. Not because they were magical or chosen, but because they were able to stay so deeply connected to the soul that ego and fear didn't cloud their vision.

If that's the soul—pure, loving, accepting—then anything that moves us away from that state is disconnection. Some call it shadow.

I didn't understand any of this early on. I just knew when I felt close to the soul and when I didn't.

What Disconnection Feels Like

Judgment disconnects you from the soul.

Cruelty disconnects you from the soul.

Hatred disconnects you from the soul.

And the same is true of what we direct inward.

If you look in the mirror and think, *I'm disgusting. I'm failing. I'm unworthy*; that too is disconnection. Those moments don't make you a bad person—they make you human. But they do create distance from who you are beneath the wounds and conditioning.

When Identity Replaces the Soul

Another way to understand disconnection is through attachment. I was glad when Gina asked whether what we often call "love" might actually be coming from the ego self.

Here's how I understand it: If it ends, it isn't the soul.

Ego-level attachment to a spouse ends when one of you leaves the body. Attachment to a role or identity ends when a life chapter shifts. But soul-level love doesn't end, because it isn't tied to form. It's free-flowing and infinite.

You can love someone's soul regardless of how they act, how they show up, or what role they play in your life. Across lifetimes, relationships change—your husband doesn't stay your husband, and your child doesn't stay your child. The roles end. The soul connection doesn't.

It's human to have attachments. It's also human to attach our identity to temporary things. But those things are not who we are.

When we attach our identity to what doesn't last, we disconnect from the soul:

- I am my career.

- I am my motherhood.

- I am my relationships.

- I am my illness.

- I am my trauma.

You are not any of those things. You are your soul.

All of those identities will fall away, as will your mind. Thoughts, memories, and intellect belong to the body's lifetime, not the soul's.

This is something people with chronic illness struggle with deeply. They say, *I'm unreliable. I'm too tired. I can't keep up.* But that's not the soul. That's the body—this specific body—with its specific limits and challenges. And this body was chosen by the soul.

Your soul isn't undependable.

Your soul isn't broken.

Your soul isn't exhausted.

The mind complicates this further, because it attaches itself to this lifetime and mistakes the story for the truth. Most of what we call "identity" is ego—not arrogance, but structure. A narrative built from distraction and survival.

We cling to roles, wounds, expectations, labels—anything that feels solid. We stay busy. Productive. Frantic. All of it keeps us from asking the deeper question: Who am I really?

What Disconnection Feels Like (continued)

The truth is, being disconnected from the soul feels normal. Disconnection is part of the distraction that makes us forget. It can look like "getting lost" in doing. Manifestations of the disconnect look like judgement of ourselves and others, chronic stress, self-criticism, and getting lost in the constant noise of life.

We drift away from the soul by identifying with what ends instead of what's infinite, by letting the noise drown out the signal.

Why Humans Get Distracted (and Why It Matters)

Humans are wired for distraction. In our human form, distraction isn't a flaw; it's part of the design. We're not shallow, weak, or failing. We were built to experience life this way.

Through the spiritual lens I subscribe to, creation wants to experience itself. To know itself in form. To feel what it is to be embodied—to love and lose, to struggle and heal, to suffer and evolve. So the soul takes on form again and again, moving through different bodies and levels of awareness across lifetimes.

Some traditions say the soul experiences millions of lives before reaching human form. Whether you take that literally or symbolically doesn't matter. What matters is the principle beneath it: Consciousness grows by experiencing everything.

From that perspective, the human experience is a chapter, not a destination. And that chapter requires distraction, because distraction creates choice.

It gives us the chance to:

- Forget, so we can remember

- Stray, so we can return

- Struggle, so we can evolve

As unnecessary or inconvenient as it may feel, the soul needs the full range of human experience. If everything were stillness and soul-awareness all the time, there would be nothing to learn. No friction. No growth. No evolution.

Even science echoes this thinking. We began as microscopic life and slowly evolved through animal forms. Some humans still operate close to those instinctual layers—you see it in aggression, impulsivity, and territorial and predatory behavior. That is placement on the arc of evolution. Others are further along that arc, and you see it in empathy, intuition, creativity, compassion, and stillness.

We are wired to:

- Be distracted

- Cycle through distraction

- Plateau, grow, and plateau again

- Evolve slowly, lifetime by lifetime

At any point within a lifetime, a person can reach a kind of soul pause—not a conscious decision, not something you choose over coffee—but a deeper "knowing" of *this is as far as I can go right now*. When that happens, growth levels off. It doesn't reverse. The next lifetime simply continues where this one left off.

Soul evolution is a slow upward spiral. That's where the phrase *healing isn't linear* comes from. You rise, level out, and rise again. Even stagnation is part of the climb. That's why distraction is built into the human form.

Distraction creates the friction needed for evolution. It gives us ego, attachment, and illusion—not as punishment, but as material to work through. It's what gives us the opportunity to choose connection over fear, and ultimately, love over all else.

From the soul's perspective, that's the point. But from the human perspective, it can feel cruel—like we're puppets in some cosmic game. Maybe we are. But it's in the distraction that awakening becomes possible. And it's through awakening that our connection to the soul strengthens.

That's where this turns back toward trauma.

Trauma is one of the strongest forces that can pull us deeper into distraction—or, just as powerfully, back into awakening.

Soul Contracts, Karma, and the Invisible Threads Between Us

I asked my friend Gina to help bring the content of this book out of me because she knows how to ask the questions that unsettle things. She knows how to stir the deeper layers, even when it stirs something in her, too. She asked me to reflect on soul contracts and how they relate to trauma.

You might be wondering, "What are soul contracts?" Where do they fit? And how do they connect to trauma and the soul?

The simplest way I can answer is this: Soul contracts are karma in motion. Not punishment and not reward. Just the energetic agreements formed through every interaction we have with another being.

When people hear the phrase *soul contract*, they often imagine something ceremonial like a cosmic handshake or a dramatic spiritual blueprint. In my experience, it's much quieter and far more constant than that. Every interaction creates a contract. Every relationship. Every act of kindness or harm. Every choice and every moment of impact.

Some contracts form without our conscious choice, such as where we're born, the culture we're raised in, or the circumstances we enter life with. These are karmic threads we inherit. We didn't sign them deliberately, but we still carry them.

Other contracts form through choice: how we treat people, how they treat us, and how we respond. Each connection builds energetic completion or unfinished business, depending on the lesson. Some contracts are brief: a passing moment, a short encounter, or a single exchange that completes itself immediately. Others last a lifetime or stretch across many.

People with large social circles often carry vast webs of soul contracts—networks of teaching, triggering, healing, and shaping one another in ways most of us don't consciously recognize.

The core soul contracts, the ones that follow us through lifetimes, the ones that feel like recognition rather than coincidence often show up as:

- Parents

- Children

- Siblings

- Spouses

- And sometimes one or two close friends who feel like siblings of the soul

These relationships aren't random. They're part of a shared karmic curriculum.

If you're wondering what karma actually is, the simplest definition I can offer is this: Karma is the result of action across lifetimes. That includes not just what we do, but what we think—something that's often overlooked. What you're experiencing now is shaped by past action, and what you choose in this lifetime continues shaping what comes next.

We tend to think the goal is to have "good" karma—easy relationships, harmonious contracts, and smooth paths. But the deeper goal is neutrality and completion. Resolution. The end of repetition. And sometimes the most powerful soul contracts are the briefest ones.

This is where the conversation becomes more delicate, and I want to name that before continuing.

When I say *soul contracts include fetuses*, I'm not speaking from politics or belief systems around birth. I'm speaking from an energetic and spiritual framework.

In my understanding, the soul doesn't always enter the body at conception. I'll use myself as an example: My soul didn't enter this body until May, and I was born in June. Sometimes the soul enters earlier. Sometimes later. Always when the conditions, parents, community, and circumstance align with what the soul came to experience.

In other cases, a soul never enters the body at all, because the lesson for those involved wasn't parenthood at that moment. None of this is a judgment on the parent, the fetus, or the choices made. These are experiences, not moral verdicts, and each carries its own lessons and growth.

A soul contract can exist for however long a soul is present in the womb, regardless of whether that presence ends in birth, miscarriage, or termination. The contract exists for the time it was meant to. The impact happens. The lesson completes. The soul moves on.

That doesn't make the experience painless or insignificant. It simply means it isn't good or bad; it just is.

As I shared this, Gina offered something deeply personal. Her mother had three miscarriages before she was born. For much of her life, Gina carried the feeling that she had to *replace* something, that she could never be enough because she was never all three. That sense wasn't just ego. It was a karmic memory.

If souls were present in those pregnancies, they were energetically connected, part of her soul web, her lineage beyond biology. They may appear again in another lifetime, or even in this one, in another form: a cousin, a niece, a friend, or someone who feels familiar without explanation.

And even if no soul was present, the karmic thread still exists, shaped by how loss was experienced and carried within the family. Again, not good or bad. Just material for understanding and growth.

Time and space aren't linear when it comes to soul connections. DNA shows us physical lineage. Soul lineage moves in all directions—past lives, future lives, sideways lives. It's interwoven.

Some of the deepest bonds and lessons come from the contracts we barely notice: the souls we meet for seconds or the ones we never meet at all.

Soul contracts aren't tidy. They aren't logical. They don't fit clean frameworks. But they help explain why certain relationships feel destined, why certain losses cut deeper, and why trauma so often happens within the relationships we're most karmically entangled with.

Trauma is activation, not punishment—a catalyst that brings the contract to the surface.

When Disconnection Feels Safer Than Truth

There were long stretches of my life where being disconnected from my soul felt more normal than feeling connected to it. That isn't just my experience; it's most people's.

Soul connection sounds beautiful in theory, but in practice it can be overwhelming. It's big. It's intimate. It can make you feel impossibly small in both the best and worst ways. Imagine trying to locate a single atom in an infinite sea.

To feel the immensity of what we actually *are* is not something the human mind is built to hold all at once. Not without preparation. That's why I believe periods of disconnection are necessary, not because they're good, but because they're protective. The psyche needs time to strengthen before it can receive that kind of input without breaking. It needs time to turn insight into wisdom through lived experience.

When the soul comes through full force, it can feel like standing in front of something ancient, enormous, and infinite. Without enough healing and grounding, that intensity can tip a person into panic, overwhelm, or even psychological destabilization. I've seen it happen. It isn't poetic. It can be dangerous.

Until not too long ago, disconnection was the norm for me. It protected me until I was ready.

But even in those disconnected years, my soul kept nudging me.Quietly and persistently.

How My Soul Broke Through

One of the first ways my soul spoke was through vulnerability—or rather, the lack of it.

For years, I believed I was being open. I shared my story. I talked about my life. I even revealed the hard parts. But my affect never cracked. I smiled through it, joked through it, and intellectualized it. I could say something devastating without actually feeling it. I mistook transparency for vulnerability.

My soul was never fooled. It kept whispering, *You're not there yet.*

It was never about doing more, saying more, or sharing more. It was about letting myself feel the truth I was speaking. Letting the armor drop just enough for emotion to move. When I finally started crying in sessions—not performative release, but real tears—I knew my soul was finally pushing through the cracks.

Another nudge came through my relentless curiosity about divinity. Every time I felt pulled toward a new faith, a new text, or a new practice, it was the soul speaking. At the time, I didn't know that. I just knew I couldn't stop searching.

I remember reading the Bible and stumbling over the phrase "the wisdom of man," wondering what it actually meant. How do you gain wisdom if you aren't meant to study what humans have written? Where is this *other* wisdom supposed to come from?

Without an answer, I kept studying—Christianity, Paganism, Wicca, Buddhism, and Mysticism. Part hunger, part frustration. There was always the same underlying feeling: *I'm supposed to understand something I can't quite reach.*

Now I know that was soul-level "memory" waking up.

The more traditions I explored, the more inner conflict surfaced. The Christian dogma in me said I was doing something wrong. The spiritual part of me said it was exactly right. What I couldn't articulate back then was simple: everything I studied was pointing toward the same truth. *It's all connected.* And my soul already knew that.

Long before I knew how to listen, my body was speaking too.

Every flare-up, every illness, and every crash were signals. Whenever I ignored myself, overgave, armored up, or pretended I was fine, my body revolted.

Sometimes it whispered.

Sometimes it screamed.

Sometimes it dragged me into a vulnerability I never would have chosen willingly.

The soul speaks through the body when the mind refuses to slow down.

And then there's nature, always my lifeline, long before I knew it.

After moving to Colorado, my husband and I would go on hikes. I felt the shift the moment the trees opened around us. One deep breath and everything fell off my shoulders. More than just relaxation, it was recognition from body to soul. My soul felt clearer outside. Calmer. Quieter. Seen.

I would breathe in the mountain air and think, *This is what I've been missing. Why would I ever stop doing this?* These moments were brief, but they were impactful. Looking back now, I can see the pattern clearly:

Knowledge → Pain → Experience → Wisdom

I needed the periods of disconnection.

I needed the trauma that splintered me.

I needed the illnesses that forced me to reconsider everything.

I needed the years of studying faiths that didn't match my inner identity.

I needed the hikes where I could finally breathe in my chest instead of my head.

The soul was always there—I was the one who needed to catch up.

Each time I softened, cracked, listened, or let myself feel, even for a moment, the connection to my soul grew stronger, less fleeting, and more embodied. Spirituality was never missing; consistency was.

Trauma as the Map, Not the Identity

People talk about trauma as if it's one single thing. It isn't. It's a spectrum, from the micro-cracks we accumulate starting in the womb to the earthquakes that strike like lightning. Trauma touched almost every layer of my disconnection from the soul. And paradoxically, it also played a role in bringing me back.

The simplest way I can explain it is this: Without darkness, you don't understand light. Without contrast, you don't have context.

If you've only ever lived in light, you don't recognize it as anything special; it's just there. But when you've known darkness, light becomes unmistakable. That's why some people who appear to have very little still radiate gratitude, joy, and resilience. They know contrast. They've been through enough to recognize what *is*.

Trauma—whether small or catastrophic—gives us contrast. It shapes our ability to recognize connection when it finally arrives. The question isn't whether trauma creates disconnection, but how deep does it go before we notice what's missing. For some, the darkness has to be profound. For others, just enough to feel the difference. In my case, it built slowly, and then materialized all at once.

Does trauma escalate disconnection from the soul? Absolutely.

If pain isn't addressed, it doesn't dissolve; it compounds. Declaring yourself "ready to evolve" doesn't stop difficult things from happening. Life doesn't reorganize itself because you had a breakthrough. Other people are still living their own wounds, their own karma, and their own shadows, and eventually it all collides with your path, whether you want it to or not.

You can be the most positive person in the world and still experience loss, illness, betrayal, and pain. That isn't pessimism; that's reality. Positivity doesn't protect us from darkness. Honesty does. And the truth is simple: You can't bypass the dark.

For much of my life, I coped by pretending nothing was happening. Head in the sand. But ignoring trauma only reroutes its impact; it doesn't stop it. When the emotional body is avoided, the physical body carries the load. Chronic illness, autoimmune flare-ups, and sudden health crises are not moral failures. They often point to unprocessed emotional weight.

My own body did this repeatedly—it carried what I refused to feel.

When you begin healing, the trauma remains, but you grow stronger alongside it. The first time my asthma spiraled in 2023, I genuinely believed I might die. I had no tools. No context. No understanding. When it happened again in 2024, I wasn't calm, but I wasn't unraveling either. The most recent flare didn't terrify me; it annoyed me. As my perception shifted and healing deepened, each episode became less violent and shorter in duration.

I'm still going to experience trauma, but spirituality prepared me for meeting the trauma differently.

I often imagine the soul like the sun behind dirty glass. You don't smash the glass clean all at once. You wipe it slowly. Therapy. Shadow work. Embodiment. Faith. Little by little, the glass grows clearer. The pain doesn't disappear, but it's seen in context. Trauma becomes something you move through, not something you drown in.

This process also changed my relationship with death. I don't want to die, but I no longer panic at the thought of it. Death is the only guarantee we get in life. Even if I healed perfectly, this body would still end one day. The vessel is temporary. The soul isn't. That understanding came from walking through enough darkness to finally recognize the light behind it.

I think often of a friend who passed from stage-four lung cancer. She radiated joy and gratitude until the end. She had done her work. She had met her shadows. Unless you knew her intimately, you wouldn't have realized how ill she was. Her spirit was stronger than the body she lived in.

That is what trauma can become when it's metabolized: not a weight, but wisdom.

I'm not fully there yet, but it's the direction I'm walking. Darkness teaches. Light reveals. Trauma opens. And the soul waits.

I used to believe trauma was the reason I couldn't connect. Now I see it differently. Trauma showed me where the connection was missing. It showed me what needed healing. It showed me where the glass was still clouded.

Trauma disconnected me from my soul, but it was also the very thing that led me back.

Where the Light Begins to Show

Real spiritual healing began for me when I started asking different questions:

Why did this hurt me?

What did it remind me of?

Where have I felt this before?

These questions became surgical tools for the soul. They cut through the surface and got straight to the root. And more often than not, the root wasn't "they hurt me."

The root of the trauma was really about how the moments of them hurting me made me feel:

Unseen.

Unsafe.

Unworthy.

This practice—getting very close to my fears and pain instead of running from them—helped me confront beliefs I'd been carrying for lifetimes. Reacting is human. Anger, defensiveness, and armor are all normal. For a long time, anger was my first response. A fiery, ready-for-battle kind of anger. But reacting from that place only fed the shadow. It added more noise. More distance.

Healing began when I learned to step back, and instead of bypassing or suppressing the fear, remove myself just enough to see clearly. Healing continued when I began recognizing *this isn't really about them. It's about what this stirred in me.* Healing lives in understanding why the wound exists in the first place.

That realization came to me as an embodied knowing through the grace of my beloved Guruji during my first Kriya Yoga retreat. Trauma doesn't exist to break you. It exists to make you conscious. I once believed trauma was proof that something was wrong with me. It wasn't. And nothing is wrong with you either. Trauma is evidence of a healing that is meant to happen. It's a map, not an identity.

This isn't meant to minimize trauma or the pain it brings. All of it is valid. All of it matters. Spiritually speaking, the deeper the wound, the deeper the wisdom waiting underneath it. The wisdom that is waiting to be discovered as part of your growth in this life.

CHAPTER SIX

From Survival To Sacredness

The Moment She Snapped Me Back Into Myself

I didn't ease my way into sacredness. I was shoved into it. By my own body.

It started during one of the worst asthma flares of my life. Asthma flares are always inconvenient, but many are a "grab the inhaler and move on" kind. Not this one. This was the kind that makes you wonder if your lungs are quietly negotiating your exit.

I had been in and out of the doctor's office so many times the nurses knew my history without opening the chart. Every visit followed the same choreography: oxygen levels, medication adjustments, more tests, more specialists, and that same tight look on my immunologist's face: carefully contained concern.

But this appointment felt different the moment he sat down. Doctors don't sit down when things are routine. They sit down when they are out of ideas or when they have important news to break.

"Heather... we really don't know what to do at this point."

He started listing specialists like he was reading from a grocery list of panic. Neurologist. Cardiologist. Pulmonologist. And then he added things to that list that we couldn't get at the panic grocery store. More imaging. More bloodwork. CT scans. Echocardiograms. Each word felt heavier than the last.

"We think this is more than asthma. Chronic asthma doesn't explain this." Then came the pause. The kind of pause that says the worst part without speaking it.

"It's not looking good."

There it was.

The sentence that rearranges your nervous system.

Great.

Fantastic.

Exactly what you want to hear when you've already been living off sheer willpower and prayer. I left that appointment wired and hollow at the same time.

Eighty milligrams of prednisone. If you've ever been on it, you know that it doesn't just treat inflammation. It lights your nervous system on fire.

My brain was running in circles while my lungs were on strike. I couldn't complete a thought. I couldn't finish a sentence. My hands trembled and my chest tightened. It felt like someone was sitting on my ribcage while simultaneously plugging my body into an electrical socket.

And still, externally, I continued to say, "I'm fine." Because that's what I did. I survived. I performed. I endured.

All the roles I had played; wife, mother, caretaker, community leader, responsible one, strong one...

None of them could breathe for me now.

None of them could step in.

None of them could fix this.

I had built an entire life around being everything for everybody. And now I couldn't even pull air into my own lungs. I couldn't breathe. Literally. And underneath the panic, something deeper was cracking.

When the body starts shutting down, it forces a question: *What have you been carrying that was never yours?*

Soon after that doctor appointment, I had a therapy session. God bless my therapist. I was visibly vibrating over the video connection—chemically wired, spiritually fractured, and physically exhausted. I was talking too fast, barely breathing, half crying, half raging, words tumbling over each other while my lungs fought for air between sentences.

It wasn't the "self-aware growth" most people imagine when they think of therapy. It was a complete collapse.

With my voice shaking and prednisone roaring through my bloodstream, I remember saying to her, "My entire life I have been everything for everybody, and now I'm dying from asthma. After everything I've lived through... I'm dying of asthma! Really! That's absolutely ridiculous."

I wasn't looking for comfort, nor was I looking for some kind of justice. I was angry. And not just a simmering resentment type of anger—this was volcanic anger. I needed to voice what I was feeling about my situation. I remember telling the therapist, "I wasted my life being who everyone else needed me to be. I wasn't even being me. And now I'm sick. And exhausted. And done."

Done. The word tasted foreign in my mouth. Then I said something to the therapist that I never thought I would say out loud.

"I want to burn the whole world to the ground."

Silence. She didn't flinch, panic, or even tilt her head in clinical concern.

She asked, evenly, "Why can't you?"

That question hit me harder than the diagnosis. *Why can't I?*

Why can't I stop contorting myself into every version that keeps everyone else comfortable?

Why can't I stop swallowing my needs whole and calling it maturity?

Why can't I stop silencing the most spiritual, intuitive parts of myself because they might make someone uncomfortable?

Why can't I stop being the quiet one while my body screams?

Somewhere between the wheezing and the rage and the chemical chaos in my bloodstream, something ancient and primal rose up. Without hesitation, the words came out of me before my fear could edit them: "Why can't I? I can. I will."

And in that moment, deep inside my chest, deeper than the asthma and deeper than the panic, something abruptly snapped back into place. There was no meditation bowl, no soft lighting, and no relaxing soundtrack. This was a soul-level ENOUGH.

I was still wired, still shaking, and still breathing like a ninety-year-old smoker with emphysema, but underneath that, something different stood up. That "something" led to questions about identity instead of survival.

Who am I really, underneath all this? Not the watered down version I let peek out in private. The real me.

Who was I before I hardened?

Who was I before I armored up?

Who was I before I swallowed myself to be palatable?

Who was I spiritually?

Fear crept in next. Not about dying, but about being seen for who I really was as a person. For being seen as me.

What would my husband think about my being more open with my spirituality? He had always tolerated my "spiritual side quests"—the sage sticks in the backyard, the Full Moon rituals, the journal tucked away in my shed.

But this was different. This wasn't a phase, or curiosity, or aesthetic spirituality. This was me stepping into the woman I had always been internally: Full and unapologetically spiritual.

My therapist said gently, "Just be honest with him. Ask."

Ask. Such a simple word.

Up until that moment, my sacred life had lived in my "she" shed, tucked away like contraband. Like something that needed to stay small in order to be tolerated. Like it needed permission to be public. And suddenly I was tired of hiding it.

After spending time sitting with the idea, without rehearsing it, without softening it, and without asking permission in my tone, I said, "I want to set up an altar inside the house."

He blinked slightly. "What do you mean, an altar?"

"Just a small shelf," I said. "A space where I can put reminders of my faith. Of who I really am."

There was a brief pause. Then he said, simply, "Sure. That's fine."

That's fine.

Years of hiding, minimizing, and negotiating my own soul came down to "that's fine."

I sat there stunned. All that fear, all that bracing, and all that internal war... for what?

The truth is the moment didn't feel calm, like some enlightened moment with violins swelling in the background. It felt messy and angry. It felt like the daunting realization that I had been the one holding the cage door shut all this time. I was angry at myself.

But I was done disappearing. Done asking permission to exist. Done translating myself into something easier for the room. I made a vow to myself: *I'm going to be who I am, even if I shake while doing it.*

That was the day survival loosened its grip. That was the day the "becoming" began. That was the day sacredness stopped being something I admired from a distance. That day, sacredness became something I would choose—daily.

The Breadcrumbs Toward Kriya Yoga

After the altar, after the anger, and after the vow to stop disappearing, something inside me had permission to breathe again. Not fully or elegantly, but enough to notice.

The first breadcrumb arrived in the form of a book: *Breath* by James Nestor. Everyone talks about that book like it's soothing, grounded, and calm. At the time, I was none of those things. I was still wired on eighty milligrams of prednisone. My nervous system felt like a live electrical wire. My lungs were unreliable. My thoughts wouldn't land.

When I picked up that book, it wasn't from curiosity. It was desperation.

"Alright, James," I remember thinking. "Tell me how to breathe. Because clearly my body missed the memo."

In one chapter he mentioned a breathing technique with a Sanskrit name—Sudarshan Kriya. He described it almost casually. Then he referenced meditating with a CD.

A CD? It was 2024. I laughed out loud and thought, *What is this, 1997?* But underneath the sarcasm, something happened.

The way he described the breath... something in me stilled. Just for a second, a flicker of calm moved through my chest, the same chest that had felt clamped shut for months.

That flicker was enough to get me from sarcastic curiosity into action. So, I did what any desperate, over-stimulated woman on the edge of either a breakdown or a breakthrough does: I Googled it.

The moment I typed the Sanskrit word, the screen filled with one phrase: Kriya Yoga. I'd done yoga before—studios, classes, flow, sweat. But this felt different. It looked different.

I clicked the first link: Kriya Yoga International.

To my surprise, something in my body reacted before my brain could. It felt like a bell had been struck inside my sternum.

I didn't know what it meant. I had no concept or understanding of the lineage the site spoke of. Heck, back then I couldn't have explained the difference between Kriya, Tantra, Hatha, Vinyasa, or a Venti Caramel Macchiato. All I knew was that it called to me. And when something calls you like that, you either lean in—or you spend the rest of your life wondering.

I kept digging, and to my surprise, there was an ashram six minutes from my house.

Six. Minutes.

An **ashram** (or asram) is a secluded, peaceful, or quiet place of spiritual retreat, hermitage, or monastery, typically associated with Hinduism and Buddhism.

There are moments in life when coincidence stops feeling random. This was one of those moments. You can call it synchronicity, divine orchestration, or algorithmic targeting, but all I knew was this: I had been gasping for breath, and something that could possibly help me, something ancient, was sitting six minutes away.

I clicked "Upcoming Events" expecting the usual—marketing, warm invitation, clear explanations, class schedules, first one free, etc..

Instead? There were a few sparse lines to read. It was almost secretive. You had to dig. Which, honestly, made it more intriguing.

Even people who practice Kriya don't really explain it. They talk about the experience. The stillness. The transformation. But not the mechanics. It felt like a spiritual Fight Club.

Rule #1: *In Kriya, we don't talk about Kriya Yoga.*

Then I saw it: "Initiation required." *Initiation? First a CD in 2024, now this?*

To my Western brain, it sounded culty. Ceremonial. Exclusive. Ominous. Yet, it didn't scare me away. In fact, it did the opposite. It made my pulse quicken in a loving, butterflies-in-the-stomach kind of way.

I later learned that initiation, "Diksha," carries a sacred meaning in traditional lineages. It refers to the formal, often one-on-one, ceremony in Hindu, Buddhist, and Jain traditions where a guru initiates a student, giving them a mantra or guidance to begin a spiritual journey. It represents preparation, commitment, and transmission.

The next initiation at this ashram wasn't for another month. A month. I remember thinking: *Will I even be alive in a month?* My body felt unstable. I was still on high-dose steroids, my breath was unreliable, and my doctor had just told me things weren't looking good.

Despite my health, my husband and I were about to leave for Oregon. I wanted and needed a couple of weeks where I didn't have to face it all. I had told my doctor I didn't want to do more tests until after this trip, and either out of compassion or pity, he agreed.

Somewhere in the back of my mind, a quiet thought whispered, *This might be our last trip together.* I genuinely didn't know how much time I had left.

Oregon was beautiful. Yet, if I'm honest, part of me wasn't there. That part of me was six minutes from home at an ashram. Waiting.

When we got back home, I looked up the date of the next initiation again. August 2024.

My hands were shaking. My breath was still ragged. And my "rational" mind was screaming. But the pull was louder than all the rest. As if something so big was indeed physically pulling me.

I registered for Kriya initiation. Then I panicked. Then I felt electric with excitement. Then I panicked again.

Life does that. It places something in front of you that terrifies you and saves you at the same time. And until you brave the fear, you can't experience the rescue.

The Trail That Led Me to Shamanism

Where Kriya opened me up in ways no other spiritual practice had ever done before or since, shamanism blew the door off the hinges to my capabilities as a healer.

The concept itself wasn't new to me. Years earlier, I'd studied Pagan traditions, Wicca, myth, and archetypes. I understood the structure of shamanic cosmology in theory. But theory had never felt personal. Not until Kriya. Not until the quiet got loud enough for me to hear myself.

I need to say this clearly: Kriya Yoga and modern shamanic practice are not the same. They do not merge. They are distinct lineages. Distinct disciplines. Distinct commitments. I respect both too deeply to blur them. But in my life, they unfolded side by side, and that is important to this story.

It was my intuitive life coach who nudged the next door open. "If you're going to do this Kriya thing," she said, "keep a journal. Ask before you meditate. Write what comes after."

It sounded simple. It wasn't. Three weeks into practice, I sat down with my notebook. I proceeded to write a question I had avoided my entire life: What is my purpose?

The answer came so fast it startled me. *Soul Healer.* I stared at the words I had written like they didn't belong to me. *"Soul Healer? What does that even mean?"* My rational mind immediately started scrambling. Dig. Research. Define. After all, digging I can handle. The search led to one word: shamanism.

Not "therapist".

Not "coach".

Not "energy-worker".

Shamanism.

I laughed. *Oh Universe, can you be subtle just once?*

But underneath the humor was recognition. The breadcrumb trail wasn't random; it was pointed. And once I saw it, I couldn't unsee it.

I continued digging into what this meant for me. The next step would be training. Less than a month away, a two-year training course in shamanism was starting. Two years. Not a workshop. Not a weekend. Two years. Lineage. Ethics. Practice. Responsibility. A discipline, one to be respected with a degree of devotion. Learning not just how to journey, but how to hold space without harming anyone. Learning not just how to see, but how to anchor.

Here's the thing about me: I don't half-step. If I'm in, I'm in.

I knew this wasn't about ego. Or some superficial title or aesthetics. Or for some cool Instagram spirituality. This was for truth.

Before fear could talk me out of it, I registered for the course. I had learned from the Kriya initiation that fear is the first step toward transformation, and I was ready to jump in.

When I stepped into that first training space? Something in me relaxed. This was the opposite of new. Because it wasn't new; it felt like remembering. Like muscle memory. Like stepping back into a room I had once lived in and somehow forgotten. I was naming something I had already been doing my entire life.

The vivid inner worlds.

The dissociation that felt like travel.

The "knowing" before knowing.

The way people confessed things to me without understanding why.

The way energy moved through a room before I even entered it.

It all made sense in a grounding and sobering way. In a way that said: You weren't broken. You were uncontained. And the deeper I went, the clearer it became: This was home.

Home.

Stepping into it wasn't about becoming something else; it was about reclaiming something that had never left. This wasn't new. This was home.

CHAPTER SEVEN

Encounters and Teachers

My First Encounter with Kriya

We'll go into my shamanic journey a bit later, but because these events were unfolding almost simultaneously, they intertwine in my memory. To fully understand what changed, we have to backtrack to Kriya.

That first Kriya initiation was slightly terrifying. I knew that this was going to change everything. I didn't know what "everything" meant yet, but my body did.

I remember sitting there trying to act normal, hands folded, posture steady, like this was just another yoga workshop. Inside, though, I felt like a kid on the first day of school mixed with a woman standing at the edge of a cliff.

It was intense. My hands were sweating. My heart wouldn't settle. The room felt enormous. The moment felt bigger than me.

This wasn't casual or mere curiosity. This felt like crossing a threshold. It was powerful, and my body knew it. This yoga wasn't flowy, flexible, aesthetic, or performative. It was precise. Intentional. Almost architectural in its design. Every breath had a reason. Every movement had a purpose.

The instructor, called a Yogacharya, began with the teachings—the structure of the practice, why each step exists, why the breath matters, why the lineage matters.

A Yogacharya is a spiritual teacher within the lineage that has been practicing a minimum of 13 years and has dedicated their lives to teaching the practice of Kriya Yoga.

As the Yogacharya spoke about the Masters guiding the practice through an unbroken lineage, I felt my Western brain quietly raise an eyebrow. Okay... sure. Let's see.

The initiation began with genuine stillness and pure presence. There was nothing theatrical or dramatic about it. No lights were dimmed. No hands were laid on me. Yet something happened. A calm so profound it felt like my entire system exhaled after decades of clenching. Like I had been dropped into the eye of a storm.

Suddenly my mind simply stopped being the loudest thing in the room; something else became louder than my thoughts.

Divinity became so full, so undeniable, that my thoughts couldn't interrupt it anymore. It was like someone had turned up the volume on something or someone I'd been straining my whole life to hear: God.

For the first time, I could *hear* God. Not with my ears or as a voice in my head. And not in my imagination. But as something much deeper: recognition. Communion. A directness that bypassed language.

There's a point during initiation that, in Christian terms, would feel similar to baptism. Not in ritual form but in intention. In choosing. In claiming. And in choosing back.

As we moved through the initiation, emotion overtook me so quickly I didn't have time to resist. I wept. It all came so naturally. There was no music swelling and nobody touching me. There was no speech that stirred me. My entire body silently and reverently participated from within.

It was as gentle and humbling as rose petals whispering blessed water across my bare toes. That's the only way I know how to describe it. It was the sensation of coming home to myself. My soul had finally had enough room to stretch and say, *I'm here.*

The feeling was pure joy and relief at the same time. It was a recognition I could never turn back on again. It was grounded power. It was steady. Nothing about it was overwhelming or destabilizing. Everything in me felt open: chest, throat, back, even my hands were buzzing. In that stillness, in that swelling of emotion, one truth settled into me with absolute clarity: *This is the place where my soul shines.*

Kriya didn't become my practice because it was dramatic, dogmatic, excitingly culty, or any of those preconceptions. It became my practice because it was true—pure truth.

I grew up praying. But prayer, for me, had always been talking. Asking. Begging. Explaining. Waiting for a sign. Chasing a feeling. Kriya taught me the other half of prayer: listening.

Kriya taught me that divinity speaks back, but not in words, commands, or visions like we are often taught. It speaks back in a quiet, embodied knowing that lands in your system and rearranges you from the inside out. And I believe, with everything in me, that this is what Jesus was doing when he went off alone to pray. We're told, "He spoke to God." But no one explains how he *heard* God. No one talks about the mechanics of communion.

After sitting inside that depth of stillness, I knew that whatever he tapped into, it felt like this. That interior listening. That direct alignment. That steady intimacy.

I'm not saying Kriya is Christianity. I'm not saying it replaces anything. I'm saying that I recognized something ancient and familiar in that silence. And that the ancient and familiar "something" brought me closer to God. Closer to Jesus. Kriya made me more devotional. And I learned that devotion isn't performance. Devotion is attention. It's breath. It's showing up daily and allowing yourself to be quiet enough to hear.

That initiation gave structure and stability to something I had always been seeking. It grounded me. It gave form to longing and devotion. What I found there was home, belonging, and sacredness in its purest form.

Sacredness is available to everyone. It isn't reserved for monasteries or mountains or saints.

You don't have to adopt my practice. You don't have to adopt my language. But if my story helps even one soul remember how to listen, how to sit long enough to feel that interior stillness, then I've been of service.

And if you take anything from this, let it be this: The sacred finds you, if you let it.

My First Encounter with Shamanism

My relationship with shamanism began with a soul retrieval and healing session I didn't fully understand at the time. I had scheduled the soul retrieval long before I knew what "soul retrieval" actually meant. I was already practicing Kriya, building my altar inside the house, slowly dismantling the version of myself that had survived by shrinking.

Still, something in me felt like it was missing. Not broken, just missing. I couldn't name it. I just knew there was a part of me I had left behind somewhere along the way. And I wanted it back.

That first session was powerful, but the true impact didn't land immediately. It was like planting something underground. I wouldn't see the roots until later.

When I attended my first "official" shamanism class, I expected fireworks. Instead, after our first group journey, I sat there thinking, *That's it?* Not because it was shallow in any way. Or because it lacked meaning. But because it felt exactly like something I had been doing my entire life, without knowing it had a name.

When I read books as a child, I didn't imagine the scenes; I entered them. I daydreamed entire worlds in vivid form. When I worked in high-risk environments and my stress spiked, I would slip into what I called "active meditation." I would create a sacred inner space while my body continued performing its duties. At the time, I thought it was imagination. Or coping. Or some strange flaw.

I didn't know it had lineage.

I didn't know it had structure.

I didn't know it had boundaries.

In that first class, we journeyed to meet our protective power animal. Journeying is a meditative technique that uses rhythmic drumming to enter an altered state of consciousness. It's used to access non-ordinary reality. Before the drumming even settled into rhythm, I knew who mine was. I had met that guide when I was fifteen during a self-created spiritual exercise. I didn't understand it then. I didn't know it "counted." I didn't know it was legitimate.

Thirty years later, there it was again, unchanged. As if no time had passed. As if it had been waiting for me to notice. This wasn't imagination; it was continuity.

After that class, I met with my intuitive life coach, who was also a licensed therapist. If anyone could help me ground this, it was her. I told her everything. The familiarity. The ease. The strange obviousness of it all. She listened carefully and then said something that reframed my entire life: "You spend a lot of your time in non-ordinary reality."

The words hit like divine truth. I didn't feel alarmed or accused. This was a truth that lived deep within me, and suddenly everything made sense.

The vivid inner landscapes.

The intuitive hits.

The way I sensed shifts before anyone spoke.

Up until then, I had been slipping into those states unconsciously. And that was the danger. Not the journeying itself. The lack of boundaries around it. When you enter non-ordinary reality without intention, it isn't spiritual practice; it's coping. If you don't know how to anchor yourself, what feels mystical can become psychologically unstable.

My intuitive coach didn't tell me to stop journeying. She taught me how to choose when to go in and when to go out. How to set energetic boundaries and how to ground afterward. She taught me how to open the doorway instead of falling through it.

That control changed everything. While others may rely on drumming to enter non-ordinary reality, I can enter that state with or without tools. I have been doing it since childhood—intuitively, naturally. Now I use the tools intentionally, even if I don't need them. They help me choose. They remind me that I am entering sacred space deliberately, not drifting there unconsciously. That is an essential distinction.

Compared to Kriya, Shamanic journeying felt lighter. Not less powerful. Just different. Kriya takes me into the deepest stillness I've ever known. Into communion with God, into listening. Shamanism feels like stepping into a landscape that was always familiar.

Kriya anchors me in divinity. Shamanism reveals my wiring. Kriya showed me the Divine. Shamanism showed me pieces of my own blueprint. One taught me how to listen to God. The other showed me how I am built to serve.

They are not the same practice. They are not blended. I honor them separately. But in my life, they arrived together as two currents of the same awakening.

One, steady and vertical. One, expansive and horizontal. Both leading me toward the same truth: I was not becoming someone new. I was remembering who I had always been.

Nature as Teacher, Mirror, and Communion

If you had asked young Heather whether nature was spiritual, she wouldn't have had the language for it. She just knew.

I always felt connected to nature. Not in a poetic, "tree-hugger" cliché kind of way. It was simpler than that. Nature was big and quiet.

She didn't need me to perform.

She didn't need me to protect her feelings.

She didn't need me to shrink.

I could stand inside something vast and not be required to be anything at all. It wasn't until much later that I realized nature had been speaking to me my entire life.

One of the most profound moments came in the least expected place, the Woodland Park Zoo. I remember standing and locking eyes with an orangutan. We were intently looking at each other when I noticed it. What most people would have interpreted as "animal emotion," I knew was grief. Bone-deep grief. The kind that settles behind the eyes and doesn't move.

The orangutan lay there, heavy, still, and withdrawn in a way that felt painfully familiar. A few feet down the enclosure, a sign explained that its companion of more than twenty years had recently died.

To say that something in my chest cracked is an understatement. This wasn't imagination or projection. This was yet another form of recognition. I didn't see "an animal feeling sad." I saw a being grieving the loss of its beloved.

That moment changed me. Once you see that we share the same emotions and the same capacity for grief and love as animals do, once you feel it, there's no going back to the hierarchy humans like to create. We are not separate from the animal world. Biologically, emotionally, and energetically we have the same building blocks. The same nervous systems that are wired for attachment. The same capacity for love and loss.

Another crack in the illusion happened many years ago in community college, during what I used to call my "wasting my parents' money" phase. I read *Ishmael* by Daniel Quinn. That book didn't just challenge my thinking; it rearranged it. It forced me to question the story humans tell about dominance, superiority, and our right to consume and control everything around us. After that, I could no longer see the natural world as background scenery. It was no longer just "resources." It was a sacred relationship.

Although these experiences opened my mind to the spirituality of the natural world, my true spiritual understanding of nature didn't fully land until later, through Kriya, through shamanism, through healing. Before, I intellectualized connection. After, I experienced it.

Now, when I say "God is," I mean exactly that. God is.

God is the tree.

God is the clouds.

God is the dappled sunlight on my skin during a hike.

God is the silence in the woods.

God is the smell of pine.

God is the dirt under my feet.

God is the deer that pauses and looks at me as if it recognizes something.

God is the dog asleep on the couch.

God is the cat purring in the window light.

Not symbolically. Literally. We are all made of the same material: protons, neutrons, and electrons. We are atoms configured differently, but sourced from the same origin.

The tree is God configured as wood and chlorophyll.

I am God configured as bone and breath.

A dog is God configured as fur and devotion.

So when I stand in nature, I am not "connecting with God" as a metaphor. I am standing within God. Within the most undistorted expression of divine energy available on this planet.

That is healing—coherent and real.

Our atoms respond to the atoms around us.

Our nervous systems co-regulate.

Our energy fields shift in the presence of other fields.

When we're around humans, shadow interacts with shadow. Trauma brushes trauma. Ego bumps ego. Wounds meet wounds.

Nature does not carry psychological shadow. Nature carries existence.

It experiences.

It moves energy through.

It sheds what is dead.

It grows toward light.

It does not cling to narrative.

That's why sitting under a tree feels different than sitting in a room full of people. That's why a nature hike can quiet a panic attack faster than a conversation. That's why standing at the edge of the ocean feels both grounding and expansive at the same time. That's why climbing to a mountain vista can drop you into communion faster than a memorized prayer.

When we meditate in nature, something amplifies. It's like tuning a guitar string to perfect pitch. Nature raises us, steadies us, and clears us. Not by trying but by being. Because God *is*. And nature is God in its simplest clothing.

You don't have to use the word "God." Call it physics. Call it biology. Call it coherence. But you can't argue with this: Your atoms recognize their source.

This is why I tell people, even the ones who think spirituality is nonsense: *go outside.*

Living More, Living Sacred

During one of our interviews for this book, Gina asked me a question that landed deeper than I expected: "Would you say you're truly living now?"

The honest answer? "I'm living *more* now." Not perfectly. Not flawlessly. Not in some floating, enlightened state where nothing rattles me and every moment glows.

As the title of this book implies, I'm married. This means there are two humans with two shadows and two karmic piles trying to love each other without reopening old wounds. In addition to my husband, my son lives with us, and my daughter and granddaughter visit often. I also see clients, work with writers, editors, and virtual assistants. And I still have a team of doctors and practitioners I continue to work with.

I still get triggered. My mind still grabs for old patterns. There are still days where the planner in me tries to run the show. Sacred doesn't mean sanitized. It means conscious.

As a soul inside a human body, I am living more now than I ever have because the way I understand who I am has changed everything. I don't walk around pretending I'm "above" humanity. I'm very aware I am human. But underneath everything, there is a steady knowing that this life is temporary, this body is temporary, and this chapter is one of many.

That awareness can go two ways: It can spiral into nihilism. "None of this matters." Or it can do what it did for me. "This is temporary; every moment matters."

That shift changed how I move through the world. Of course, I still slip. Future Heather still tries to take over—the fixer, the strategist, the one who wants guarantees. Even during this book process, I feel that tug. But underneath it is a steady voice reminding me to stay here and to stay present.

This moment is the only one that's real. And when you really understand that, not intellectually, but in your bones, you live differently.

I talk to the grocery store clerks like they matter. Because they do. I tell people I love them when I feel it. Not casually; I mean the kind of love that sees the divinity in them and honors it. I pause long enough to notice sunlight on my skin and the way my dog breathes when she sleeps. I notice the exact texture of a quiet moment.

To all these experiences, I whisper thank you. Every interaction carries intention now. What you see is who I am. Not a curated version and definitely not a persona. Just me—present, flawed, and learning.

Gina asked if this was "sacred living." Not exactly. For me, it's closer to "living a sacred life."

Sacredness already exists. It's not something we create. It's something we align with. Living a sacred life is choosing devotion, not as dogma but as orientation. It's choosing to see divinity everywhere: in others, in myself, in conflict, and in forgiveness. It's remembering that my voice isn't just mine.

That my choices ripple. That I am part of something larger than this single lifetime.

When I think of sacred living embodied fully, I think of Jesus. I think of the Dalai Lama. I think of my beloved Guruji, Paramahamsa Prajnanananda. People who are so immersed in divine awareness that when they speak, it no longer feels separate from God.

They're called self-realized or God-realized not because they float above humanity, but because they are anchored so deeply in communion that the line between human and divine softens. A true Master will always acknowledge their humanity. They will invite questions. They will not demand devotion. They will never need worship. They share wisdom. They share love. That's how you know it's not culty.

This book is not me claiming that level of realization. It's me walking toward it.

My path has been paved with forgiveness. Forgiving the angry, hardened, silent version of me. The woman who chose survival over truth. I've forgiven others, not by erasing what happened but by seeing their divinity under their damage.

And the hardest forgiveness of all: *Forgiving my soul for choosing this life.* For choosing lessons that cut deep. For choosing experiences that shaped me through fire. That is the hardest work I've done in this incarnation.

I remember the first time I did a cord-cutting and genuinely felt love for the person I was releasing. A cord-cutting is a spiritual practice of releasing the energetic ties we hold to people or experiences—especially those rooted in pain, attachment, or unresolved emotion. For years I had joked, "I return this garbage to sender with love." But that day, the love was real. The forgiveness was real. A raw, visceral forgiveness that permanently unclenched something in me.

So am I living a sacred life? Yes and no. Yes, because I am committed, moment by moment, to authenticity and compassion. No, because I am still human. But I am closer than I have ever been to living a sacred life. And that means something. Whether I have 109 more lifetimes or four, this life moved the needle.

My glass is clearer than it was. That is faith, not belief. Belief is what you are told. Faith is what you experience. What you experience reinforces faith. What you integrate becomes wisdom. None of this belongs to me. These truths echo across cultures and centuries because they are lived, not invented.

My story is simply one more expression of something ancient. It's ordinary. I wasn't raised in a monastery. I didn't grow up in a yogic lineage.

I came from:

- Trauma.

- Corrections work.

- Asthma.

- Marriage.

- Divorce—twice.

- Parenting.

- Chaos.

And still, here I am on a path I never expected, yet somehow always belonged to.

CHAPTER EIGHT

Unbinding Trauma

When I think about going deeper into trauma—mine, yours, any-one's—the first thing that comes to mind is that glass we talked about earlier. How healing isn't one big revelation but a slow, steady wiping away. A clearing. A loosening. A softening of what's been hardened for years and, in some cases, lifetimes.

For most of my life, I tried to heal everything fast. Push through. Power through. Overcome. That's how you survive trauma when you're young; you move fast because if you slow down, it catches you. But healing should be the opposite. Healing asks you to slow down enough to feel. And that's where things get complicated.

This body (*any* human body) can only handle so much at once. Trauma binds itself into the muscles, the fascia, the organs, the nervous system, and so on. If or when you try to tear it out all at once, it just tightens its grip even further. Healing is not a sprint. It's not a shaman session, a retreat, or a single awakening moment. It's a lifetime commitment to softening what trauma has made rigid. I learned that the hard way, and my hope in sharing my story is that you don't have to.

There were so many times I wanted to be "done." I wanted to walk into a healer's office, lie on the floor, purge out every wound I'd carried, and walk away enlightened. Trauma doesn't work like that. And neither does the soul. My therapist used to remind me that you can't force your way into healing. You can only allow it.

There are layers, much like scar tissue, around an old surgery. Old patterns wrapped around old pain. When you finally begin tearing those layers apart, the emotions underneath don't come out all at once. They rise in waves—sadness, anger, memories, insights—and your body has to integrate each one.

Sometimes the release isn't even emotional; sometimes it's an epiphany. A piece of clarity you didn't even know you were reaching for. A moment where the soul can finally speak because the body and mind are no longer guarding the door.

That's why going "deeper into trauma" is never a single act. It's a rhythm. A cycle of: Uncover → feel → rest → integrate → repeat. Each time the cycle resets, something loosens.

I used to think I could bypass that process with one practice, a few healing sessions, or a couple of retreats, but I now know better. You can't just go to a shaman once, join that fancy yoga/meditation retreat, or drink the plant medicine and blow open the door. While all these things help, they all mean nothing if you come back home and go right back into the same unconscious patterns you've been living. The door may open, but you still have to walk through it, step by step.

You cannot rush the unbinding of trauma in the body. The soul can't reconnect through force. Healing takes the time it takes. And it takes faith, not in a belief system, but in the body's quiet wisdom to release what you're finally strong enough to face.

The Anchors of My Story

During our interviews for the making of this book, I was asked what my "anchor traumas" were, the ones that stay lodged in your system. For many of us, these patterns happen immersively, and so often, you stop recognizing them as trauma. They become part of the atmosphere you live in or grew up in.

For me, one of the biggest anchors was the constant sense of unsafety. As a child, I learned early that my body wasn't mine. While there were moments of assault that carved deep grooves I spent decades trying not to look at, this knowing wasn't in the "catastrophic sense" but in the quiet, chronic way that steals your baseline safety before you're old enough to name it.

Another anchor trauma was the silencing of my intuition. I was born sensitive. Empathic. A child who felt everything before I understood anything. But in my world, sensitivity was punished, mocked, or dismissed. I learned to bite back what I sensed. To distrust the things I felt in my gut. To swallow the knowing that rose in my chest. Eventually, that silencing becomes its own trauma.A slow suffocation. A betrayal of the self so familiar that you don't notice when it becomes normal.

And then there was violence. The "corrective" kind when I was little and the controlling, manipulative kind that pervaded my life until I consciously chose to build a life that didn't revolve around it and excluded from my orbit those who perpetuated the violence. Both types carried the same message: "Your compliance is required; your feelings are irrelevant." Being hit as a child and being hit as an adult are different experiences, but they carry the same wound: *My safety depends on someone else's mood.*

I feel like I've walked through life holding death's hand.

Most humans experience death and grief. For me, those were layered on top of my anchored trauma. In a way, the amount of loss I experienced at a young age affected me more than I ever admitted. As humans, the minute we're born, we're dying. It's part of life on Earth, and yes, it's something we all have to deal with. But not everyone becomes fluent in grief before they're old enough to vote.

The Empath Trauma

To feel everything—your pain, their pain, the unspoken tension in a room, the lingering sadness in someone's eyes—is both a gift and a wound. When you have no boundaries and no guidance, empathy is not a superpower; it's an overload. It's a lifetime of emotional static that makes it impossible to distinguish your own sorrow from someone else's.

During the making of this book, when I was prompted to "Go back." My body knew where we were going. But when asked to go back to a moment where punishment or assault or fear took root, my mind didn't go to a single scene. It went to all the familiar feelings. I felt the tightening of my belly, the quieting of my breath, the instinct to shrink, and the fear of speaking, feeling, being too much.

These ingrained traumas weren't isolated incidents. They were ecosystems— the water I swam in and the air I breathed (or couldn't breathe). The quiet, repetitive shaping of a child who learned too early that her safety, her voice, and her intuition were negotiable. Trauma was the background music to an entire childhood and continued as the theme music for most of my adult life. Unbinding from it all requires going back gently and slowly, one layer at a time, not recreating scenes but reclaiming the self that was split inside those scenes.

The Moment That Lives in the Body

Since there were no isolated traumas in my childhood, when asked to go back to "one of those traumatic moments," my mind landed on a composite, a memory that isn't one event but an entire atmosphere. Everything was accumulated—layered and stacked until it became one seamless string of memories that lived in my nervous system.

When I go back, I don't see one night, one day, or one moment. I see the pattern. I see myself at around fifteen (though it could have been thirteen, or ten, or eight) walking through the front door five minutes past curfew. Some nights five minutes late meant nothing. Other nights, five minutes late meant stepping into a storm you didn't know was coming. The rules in our house weren't rules. They were roulette.

If my stepdad had been drinking, which was often, the whole energy changed. I learned to read the air before I even looked at his face. I'd walk in, and before I could even shut the door, he'd be in front of me: close, towering, jaw set. He never spanked us; he said we were "little girls" and that it "wasn't appropriate." But that didn't stop him from repeatedly thumping two fingers into the center of our chest so hard it felt like he was trying to pin our ribs to our spine.

That gesture, those two fingers, became its own language: You're in trouble. You're disrespectful. You should be afraid. He'd lean in, yell into my face, and repeatedly drill those fingers into my sternum. Even now, I can clearly sense it all: the smell of alcohol, the sharp heat of his breath, and the tension in his shoulders. Going to my room wasn't enough; a fistful of my hair was usually grabbed as I passed by, as if that would guide me. Sometimes a hard kick on my backside, not with an open hand—that would be "inappropriate"—but the tip of his shoe or foot was acceptable.

I remember that hallway more than the room. The carpet, dim light, and that feeling of bracing... shoulders up, breath tight, trying to move quickly enough not to make it worse.

As I describe this so plainly, none of it seems "catastrophic," and that's the trap. When something happens hundreds of times, it stops looking like trauma and starts being "normal." Yet all those "normal" moments created the architecture of my adult self.

The architecture:

Oppositional defiance as survival: My entire system slams on the breaks when told what to do. Even if it's good for me, even when it makes sense, my body still flinches, and my mind still rebels.

Rigid rule following to avoid unpredictability: When you never know which version of someone is waiting for you, the only safety is perfectionism. When rules keep shifting, you overcorrect.

Emotional suppression: "Wipe that look off your face before I wipe it off for you." Showing any signs of fear made things worse. The fear didn't magically disappear; it went inward. Into my muscles, my lungs, and my stomach. Silence became armor.

Stolen autonomy: When your body, your movement, is taken away—when it's no longer yours—it takes years to unravel this form of trauma. It takes commitment and work to take your power back. Having your hair yanked to pull you back or your back kicked to push you forward may not seem that bad compared to what some people have survived.

But trauma is not measured in broken bones. It's measured in repetition, in the slow erosion of safety, over and over. It's measured in the years you spend anticipating someone's mood or bracing for the impact of something you can't predict. It's measured in what it becomes inside you.

This was the environment where my body learned to armor up. Where my voice learned to disappear and my spirit learned to split. "Outer" Heather performed compliance. "Inner" Heather retreated somewhere deep. Inner Heather, real Heather, now Heather, stayed hidden, waiting for a safer life. A life that wouldn't come for a long time.

This was a part of my disconnection, not just from safety, but from myself, my intuition, and eventually my soul.

Sexuality, Boundaries and the Early Wounds That Shape Us

When asked to return to certain parts of my story, I knew we'd have to approach it the way memory itself approaches trauma—indirectly, through sensation, fragments, and the emotional imprint that remains after the mind has sealed off the specifics.

There are stretches of my childhood and early adolescence missing. It's the kind of absence that happens when the nervous system needs to shut the door in order to survive. I recall the "before" and the "after" around certain periods and events, but not the actual middle.

While I don't have the frame-by-frame images, I have context: As a child, adults around me were unsafe. There were guests in our home who were later legally charged for abusing their own children and individuals who made comments toward me that no child should ever hear.

The body remembers what the mind protects you from.

In my later childhood years bordering on the early teens, I found myself in environments where adult supervision was questionable at best. Most of us were far too young to be around drinking, drugs, older kids, and situations that blurred boundaries. Nothing about it was handled with care. Things happened in those environments, things I didn't understand at the time, not until years later. What I did understand was walking away feeling wrong inside my own skin, ashamed, and convinced that I "should have known better," even though I was a child in a situation I never should've been placed into.

By the ripe age of sixteen, the pattern intensified in the form of the teenage boyfriend I mentioned earlier, who didn't understand the meaning of "no." As a young woman sick with asthma and barely able to breathe, instead of concern, I was met with pressure and entitlement. Things quickly escalated into physical aggression. Conditioned to normalize chaotic environments, I didn't know how to leave. I didn't know how to protect myself. I didn't comprehend being allowed to protect myself.

"Children's talent to endure stems from their ignorance of alternatives."

– Maya Angelou, *I Know Why the Caged Bird Sings*

None of this is easy to share, nor pleasant to read, but it shaped what followed me into adulthood: Sex became a separate category from intimacy.

That early wiring taught me that closeness with men wasn't safe and that affection disappeared without warning. It taught me that desire was something people took, not something they shared. I came to believe that intimacy had nothing to do with actual connection.

This faulty wiring created real challenges in my life. When you grow up believing sex is transactional, a negotiation of power, something you "manage" rather than something you *feel*, it becomes impossible to understand the deeper emotional language that intimacy requires. Intimacy as closeness, not just as an intimate act.

A note on sexuality

While I consider myself a woman, this type of trauma can occur to any human being, regardless of your gender, and/or how you identify. Male, female, trans, bisexual, asexual, heterosexual, homosexual, trauma and the way any given trauma affects you, has nothing to do with your sexuality and/or sexual orientation.

Now, as a woman navigating menopause, when the body naturally changes its needs and responses, I'm facing a new kind of reckoning. If desire isn't there, what does closeness look like? How do you build intimacy when the old wiring never linked intimacy and sexuality in the first place?

This is where the healing is happening now. Not in removing the past, but in understanding it. Healing means gently unwinding the knots and learning new ways of being in relationship—with my body, with my partner, and with my soul. I now understand that sexuality is temporary. Sexual desire is necessary until it becomes a distraction or a source of pain. Sexual identity is temporary and can also become a distraction if we attach trauma to it. I am learning how to love and be loved for the soul that resides within, not for the temporary motivations of the vessel. How to love and be intimate in a way that is pure and eternal and apart from desire and ego.

Soul Memory, Gender, Sexuality, and Compassion

From the soul's perspective, identity is fluid. The soul itself carries no gender. Across lifetimes, it inhabits male bodies, female bodies, and bodies that exist outside those distinctions. With each life, memory accumulates.

For many people, those memories remain dormant. For others, fragments rise to the surface, not as clear recollections, but as sensations, attractions, longings, or dissonance within the body.

Attraction is not always sexual. Often it is a type of recognition. A deep pull toward another person may reflect a bond forged across lifetimes, one that transcends gender or form. What feels confusing in the present is frequently ancient familiarity resurfacing.

When a person feels misaligned with their body or identity, this does not indicate that something is broken. It suggests memory without language. The harm then arises not from the experience itself, but from the trauma imposed by others when that experience is judged, denied, or punished.

Our responsibility—to children, to loved ones, to one another—is not to resolve these experiences for others, but to refrain from creating additional wounds around them.

Compassion interrupts karmic repetition.

Judgment perpetuates it.

When we respond with acceptance rather than fear, we prevent trauma from being carried forward into another life, another body, and another generation.

CHAPTER NINE

The Wounds That Cut Deepest

Which wounds cut deepest? Childhood, adulthood, relationships, betrayal, illness?

All of them. And none of them.

Trauma is not one thing, one cut, one wound, one instant, one shock, one pain, or one moment. The depth of its impact isn't measured only by when it happened or even how it happened. Its impact is in how it affects you and how you store it.

Trauma can come in many shapes and forms. There is the kind that repeats, the kind that erodes you slowly and accumulates. And there is the kind that strikes like lightning, that shakes your being and brings you to your knees. All its forms can change you on a cellular level, but they carve differently.

In my case, it was the repetitive kind: the daily erosion of safety, the unpredictable explosions, the environment where my nervous system never fully exhaled. The harms that came not from one event but from living from a place of experience that trained my body to expect harm. Layer over layer, year after year, until my system adapted not just psychologically but physically as well.

The childhood volatility, the dynamics inside my first and second marriages, my divorces, the years working in law enforcement and inside a jail—all were environments that constantly pulled my body into fight-or-flight and never let it fully return. None were one-time events; they were patterns. Patterns that left their fingerprints everywhere.

This isn't to say sudden tragedies don't cut just as deep. Of course they do. Losing a child. A single moment of devastation. A tragedy. Any kind of grief that arrives without warning and rearranges the architecture of your life in an instant—all are trauma. All affect your physical and nonphysical being. There's no need to, nor can you "compare" these kinds of pain; they're different species of the same root.

When I say my deepest wounds came from repetitive trauma, I'm not saying other wounds are lesser. What embedded itself most deeply in my body were the traumas that arrived again and again until my system accepted them as the norm. And then it didn't.

The many sudden deaths I've grieved didn't create the same depth of internal scarring as the recurring traumas. There were periods of intense grief that cut deep, but they didn't create the same entrenched, long-term imprint on my health that the repetitive patterns did. For me, it was this "slow-growing" type of trauma that led my body into illness.

Every and all trauma is real, every and all trauma changes you, and every and all trauma requires healing. Trauma is trauma. Every version requires tending, witnessing, and repair.

Emotions and Mind - Their Role in Healing

If you'd asked me even as recently as a year ago what emotions would rise up when talking about my trauma, what showed up strongly were anger and fear. Anger was easier to hold. Fear was harder to name. I learned to mask one with the other. Anger felt powerful. Fear felt vulnerable. Vulnerability was never a safe space for me. Today, as I revisit my story with my current level of awareness and seat of consciousness, the emotions are different. I no longer drop back into old feelings. I'm not reliving the fear or the anger.

What do I feel now? Compassion. Compassion for the younger version of me who was trapped in those moments with no way out. I feel compassion, not just for the emotions she had to carry, but for her. Like witnessing a younger sibling or child go through something painful. You don't become their fear; you feel the tenderness of wanting to protect them.

Emotions in general, I now experience differently. I've come to see them as temporary expressions of the mind, not indicators of who I truly am. My soul, the deeper "I," doesn't experience fear.

Fear is a survival mechanism, not a truth. The ability to experience fear was gifted to us to help us understand the difference in danger between a length of rope and a snake or a tiger. It was never meant to be an emotion that we give free room and board in our minds and allow to stay there rent-free for long periods of time.

When a big emotion shows up now, the deeper, quieter voice knows to interfere. If that big emotion is fear, it asks, "Are we in danger?" The answer is usually no. This doesn't mean I suppress these emotions. A big part of healing is learning to feel emotions fully. But now they move through quickly, because I no longer mistake them for identity or truth. The emotional wave rises. And then dissolves. What does this all have to do with healing?

Healing boils down to understanding three core things:

#1 - No emotion is "bad."

Every emotion we feel is part of the human experience. Sadness, fear, anger, joy, frustration, excitement, disgust—all are signals meant to keep us safe or alert us to something unresolved. When you remove the judgment, you remove half the suffering.

#2 - The mind has a choice.

The mind is as powerful as they come, but the "I" that is "You" has a choice. Thoughts come and go and get created and diffused. When an emotion hits, the mind can cling to it, build stories around it, or let it pass through without attachment. It requires practice and work, but you can train your mind to let things pass through.

Most emotional spirals aren't about the current moment; they're about all the old impressions stacked beneath it. One situation today can activate a dozen old memories or scars. The current reaction is rarely about what is happening; it's about what already happened.

Healing means asking:

- Is this emotion coming from the present?

- Is it echoing something older?

- Where have I felt this before?

Usually when an old memory or pattern rises, it's coming from childhood, adolescence, or another period of vulnerability. Once you see the origin clearly, the emotion starts to soften.

#3 - Healing happens in layers—body, mind, and soul.

Once you've done a certain level of emotional work, awareness work, and shadow work, you realize deeper work will inevitably follow.

- Soul-level work (like guided regressions, inner child work, soul retrievals) brings back the parts of you that stepped away for protection.

- Body-level work helps address the places trauma settled in muscles, fascia, breath, and the nervous system.

- Deep meditative work helps clear the energetic pathways that strong emotions cling to or used to occupy.

The mind and body are always collaborating to heal you. They send signals, they surface memories, and they stir emotions. Not to overwhelm you, but to give you another opportunity to integrate the healing, the emotions, and the information learned from the experience. Healing compounds just like trauma does. Each layer you process opens the door to the next. As healing progresses, emotions move differently.

When a soul piece returns through healing work, it doesn't bring the damage; it brings its original wholeness. Instead of retraumatizing yourself, you reconnect to the resourcefulness, strength, and clarity that part of you always held.

Over time, triggers lose their force. The body softens. The emotional waves become quieter. Your inner reactions become more measured, intuitive, and rooted. Emotions start guiding you instead of defining you.

The Subconscious, the Body, and the Layers Between Soul and Self

When we look at the ways the human system tries to protect us, we have to note that it can also unintentionally keep us looping in the same patterns.

This is the part where science, psychology, spirituality, and the human experience all intersect.

At the very center of who we are is Pure Consciousness: the soul in its most unfiltered, unconditioned state. That core is untouched by trauma, untouched by fear, and untouched by the human story. It is simply awareness and love.

Between that core and our everyday experience of being human, there are many layers. And like sheets of glass, each one a little darker or more clouded than the last. Together, they create the "filter" through which our consciousness shines.

From closest to the soul and outward, the layers look like this:

- Pure consciousness: The eternal essence. Pure, clear light.

- Ego: The layer that gives us a sense of "I" in this lifetime. The structure that allows us to function as individuals.

- Intellect: The thinking, evaluating, analyzing part of us. Where we store learned knowledge.

- Mind: Not the brain, but the subtle body that holds impressions, emotions, and memories. The warehouse of unprocessed experiences.

- **Prana:** The energy system that animates the physical body. The conduit between the physical and subtle levels.

- The physical body: The vessel through which we live, move, sense, and experience this life.

As each layer gets more clouded by experiences, repeated stress, fear, or trauma, the light of pure consciousness has a harder time reaching us clearly. This is why intuition can feel "blocked," why emotions can feel overwhelming, and why trauma can distort how we see ourselves and the world.

What Is the Subconscious?

The subconscious isn't just one thing; it's the entire grouping of those middle layers:

- Ego

- Intellect

- Mind

- Prana

Everything between the soul and the physical body.

It's the place where:

- impressions accumulate

- memories (from this life and others) get stored

- trauma leaves residue

- intuition tries to break through

- old patterns replay until they're healed

- emotions manifest

The subconscious *can* access pure consciousness, but the signal gets refracted through all the layers. The more unprocessed impressions we carry, the more refraction there is.

Pure consciousness shines when everything else quiets down. That's why intuitive dreams, insights, or symbolic messages often come when we're sleeping. When the intellect rests, the mind slows down, and the energy system isn't distracted.

But in waking life, we can access those same intuitive signals if we learn how to quiet the noise. We quiet the noise through meditation, breathwork, stillness, nature, and practices that shift the nervous system.

When the mind quiets, the "light" gets clearer. Even if it's still passing through distortion, the clarity increases.

How Trauma Distorts the Lens

Every experience leaves an impression on the mind.

Trauma leaves heavier, denser impressions, like fingerprints smudging the glass. And repeated trauma (or long-term stress) builds up like layers of soot.

These impressions tend to distort intuition and trigger emotional reactions long after the event. They also create subconscious patterns meant to protect us but instead reinforce limiting beliefs and cause the body to hold tension or pain in specific places. They influence fears, behaviors, and defenses, shaping the way we interpret new experiences.

This is why two people can experience the same situation and have completely different reactions. One person is responding to this moment combined with all their previous impressions, and another is responding to this moment plus the twenty similar moments it reminds their subconscious of.

A Bridge to Past Impressions

Not all trauma impressions come from our current experience or lifetime. The reactions that feel "too big" or "too sudden" often trace back through:

- childhood conditioning

- preverbal experiences

- ancestral patterns

- soul-level impressions carried forward (from a past life)

These deeper impressions don't come as clear memories; they often surface as instinct, phobias, irrational fears, déjà vu, or emotional responses that make no logical sense.

This is why healing requires more than cognitive understanding. You can't reason your way out of a subconscious pattern that wasn't created through reasoning.

Why the Human Body Speaks First

The body is often the first part of us to signal that something needs attention. When trauma impressions stay stored in the subconscious for too long, the system becomes overloaded.

These cries for attention can show up as:

- chronic tension

- fatigue

- pain patterns

- inflammation

- stress responses

- emotional reactivity

- difficulty healing

- illness

The body is not "failing." It's trying to communicate. The body becomes the messenger when the mind avoids the message. It becomes the voice when emotions get suppressed and the subconscious is overloaded. When the soul is trying to guide us but can't get through the distortion, pain, illness, agitation, and burnout are often signals that the body, mind, and soul are out of alignment.

Clearing the Glass

The healing journey is really about clearing the glass. When we heal through therapy, meditation, somatic work, spiritual practices, or any mix of modalities, we are wiping one layer of the glass. Then another layer, then another, gradually allowing more of the pure consciousness to shine through.

It's slow.

It's layered.

It's deeply compassionate work.

Healing is not about becoming someone new; it's about clearing the way back to who you've always been.

How Trauma Rewires the Brain and Body

This isn't a topic I've just studied. I've lived it. Repetition rewires us. It is why "confirmation bias" exists. When the mind sees something over and over again, it begins to accept it as truth. Not because it's inherently true, but because it's familiar.

Trauma works the same way. If you repeatedly experience a threat or a *perceived* threat, your nervous system begins to treat that pattern as the world's baseline. It becomes the assumed reality.

Our bodies are incredible machines, but they're also pretty literal. Your body doesn't know the difference between a current danger and something that reminds them of a danger. And the body can't tell the difference between past and present. The body's threat-response system (the fight/flight/freeze/fawn/tend/befriend mechanisms) was built for survival in the wild.

In nature, here's what would happen:

1. A threat appears.

2. Stress hormones flood the system.

3. The body reacts—shaking, crying, running, freezing—discharging the energy.

4. The danger passes.

5. The body resets.

Animals do this instinctively. They complete the stress cycle. Whether they do it by shaking, puking, or pooping, they instinctively know to release the stress. Humans, however, don't work the same way. Humans get stuck in our modern life threats. Humans get held up in all those in-between layers of the mind, ego, and intellect. In modern human life, the "threats" are quite different:

- a hostile work environment

- social media

- watching the news

- politics

- pressure from family

- emotional stress

- carrying an entire family's emotional load

- true crime shows and podcasts available 24/7

- constant alertness

- driving in rush hour traffic

- unresolved conflict

- fear of disappointment or of not being enough

- childhood patterning

- memory of past experiences that were never emotionally processed

The body doesn't distinguish between "I'm not safe at this moment" and "I feel stressed because of a deadline." To the nervous system, it all feels the same. But unlike animals, humans rarely allow the emotional discharge that completes the stress cycle.

Instead of trembling, crying, releasing, or resting, we tell ourselves things like:

"I don't have time for this."

"Get over it."

"I have to stay informed."

"If I don't do it, it won't get done."

"This is how I decompress."

"Just push through."

"Hold it together."

And the body obeys, not because it understands, but because it's trying to keep you functioning.

The Stress Cycle That Never Completes

When the body rises into a threat response but never gets the chance to come down from it:

- stress hormones linger

- muscles stay tense

- digestion slows

- inflammation rises

- the nervous system becomes hyperalert

- the immune system gets confused

- the brain rewires toward danger-based thinking

It's like getting stuck at the top of a roller coaster with no way down.

Over time, this creates physical wear on the body. This wear, that may be "easily" prevented, eventually shows up in the form of disease. When that stress cycle is interrupted and doesn't complete for years, the body speaks. It protects you. The only way it knows how to get your attention at that point is to shout.

The body doesn't understand when we dismiss the repetitive stress, so it shouts at us through challenges such as chronic fatigue, digestive issues, autoimmune responses, hormonal imbalances, tension patterns, recurring pain, and cardiovascular strain. When the mind and the ego take over is when we tell ourselves all those untruths about being fine, being able to ignore the symptoms, or the symptoms being no big deal. The body doesn't understand. All it knows is that it rose into activation and never completed the arc. The unreleased energy gets stored in joints, muscles, fascia, the gut, the throat, the chest, the brain—anywhere the body can hold it. This is how trauma begins living in the body.

Repeated stress and fear condition the brain to anticipate danger, even when danger isn't present, so trauma survivors often live in a state of hypervigilance, shutdown, emotional numbness, or a mixture of all three. The brain learns: Safety isn't guaranteed, so stay ready. The nervous system begins to operate in survival mode, sometimes for decades.

How do I know? My body carried years of accumulated stress responses from:

- an unpredictable childhood

- emotionally volatile environments

- unsafe dynamics

- long-term alertness

- repeated patterns in adulthood

- working in high-intensity careers

The result wasn't "just emotional." It showed up in my organs, my hormones, my energy levels, my autoimmune issues... the list is long. One way or another, the body finds the way to get its message through. My healing began only when I stopped telling the body it was fine and started listening to what it had been holding.

Listening Before the Body Screams

How do you start recognizing symptoms as something deeper? How do you move past "Here's a diagnosis; take this prescription"? The real question is: How do you learn to listen before your body has to shout? How do you build enough awareness to notice the whispers before they turn into a full-blown alarm?

Here's the first thing I had to understand: Sometimes your body is just being a body.

If you understand how a healthy body is designed to function, the contrast becomes obvious. You get a cut, it bleeds, it scabs, it heals. You catch a cold, your system fights it, you rest, you recover. For the most part, your body is built to repair and regulate. When something doesn't resolve, when it keeps returning, escalating, spreading, or lingering, that's when I start paying careful attention with curiosity and honesty.

There are places where modern, Western medicine reaches a line and says, "We don't fully know why this is happening." Chronic symptoms. Pain without a clean origin story. Illness that doesn't match what your labs say you "should" be experiencing. That's where the deeper work begins. Not instead of medical care, but alongside it.

I need to state this clearly: Modern medicine is not the enemy. I'm not anti-Western medicine. If you break something, if you get an infection your body can't fight, if you're at a point where intervention is necessary, the intervention is a tool. It's a gift, not a moral failing. But a lot of people don't have the luxury of choosing between natural medicine and traditional medicine. By the time they're listening, the body is already at the end of its patience. I needed both. I let medical care take me as far as it could take me, and then I met it there with natural healing.

That "meeting it there" looks like sitting in your body, quietly, without performing, without forcing answers, and asking, *What are you trying to tell me?*

Sometimes the answer is: *I'm grieving.*

Sometimes it's: *I've been silencing myself for years.*

Sometimes it's: *I've been carrying stress like it's normal.*

Sometimes it's: *I don't feel safe.*

And the part that matters just as much as what your body is saying— is what you're saying back to it.

My body whispered long before it screamed. I think most bodies do. This shows up physically, but it also shows up mentally. We separate "mental health" like it's not the body, but it's still physiology. It's still the nervous system. It's still chemistry, pattern, and survival.

One of the most practical things I did, and still do, is get methodical. I take inventory. When I go to a medical doctor, I'm methodical about symptoms.

When I work with a spiritual practitioner, I'm just as methodical because I believe the symptoms are connected. Same body. Same signals. Two different lenses.

I track what's happening: sleep, tension, breath, energy, heartbeat, headaches, digestion, inflammation, sensitivity, and the weird little changes you're tempted to ignore because they don't "sound serious." I'm not listing every detail to a doctor like a spreadsheet of doom. Honestly the medical doctors don't have the time for that. But I'm building awareness so I can see the patterns and give them somewhere to reveal themselves.

An important part of awareness is understanding that you can't hear your body if you never let it speak. If you can't sit for five minutes without noise, without input, without something filling the space, then you won't hear the message. That prized piece of information comes only when you let it.

A simple test: when was the last time you drove without music, a podcast, an audiobook, or talking on the phone?

When it's quiet, your mind starts talking. If your inner world isn't a safe place, you'll do anything to avoid being alone with it; constant stimulation allows numbing. This is where "mindlessly" scrolling social media comes in. Where "busy" becomes an identity. And that identity belongs to the ego—not your body, not your soul.

You don't have to start this journey with a big dramatic entrance. Your starting point doesn't have to be a 10-day Bali retreat, or a two-hour meditation, or some perfect spiritual routine every morning.

Maybe it is just taking three long, slow, and deep breaths, then increasing to ten. Or taking that silent drive the next time you go out. Perhaps you leave your phone at home the next time you go for a walk.

That "alone" quality time is a form of meditation. It's a way of telling your nervous system: *I'm here. I'm listening. We are safe. We don't need to run.*

Your healing journey, reconnecting to your body and your soul, is more about the everyday little commitments that add up over time.

A moment of full disclosure, and I have to laugh at myself a little as I share this.

In the beginning, my mind tried to turn spirituality into a performance sport. Yes, that is one of my patterns: *I must be the best at everything, and in record time.* I had this ridiculous internal competition: *I'm going to become the best meditator to ever meditate.* Like someone was going to hand me a trophy for hitting a new "high score." That was my mind doing what it does—trying to control, trying to achieve, and trying to win.

And a thank you to my friend Gina for not only pointing it out but helping make this point: *You can still be human and embark on your own healing and spiritual journey.* You can still be a spouse, a parent, a business owner, someone with a demanding job, or someone who feels like they're drowning in responsibility. You don't have to disappear from life to heal, but you do need to be radically honest with yourself. And it's important to understand that this path will change you.

Know that comparing yourself to someone else's healing is just another trap. Everyone experiences the shifts differently. Things come at different timelines and different intensities, and it's entirely possible you were already working on this same healing in a prior life. Healing isn't a competition. Nobody is passing out gold medals for enlightenment.

The work is hard. Sometimes it cracks you open. Sometimes you're in the middle of it and you can't see the "better" yet; you can only feel the rawness. Sometimes you need a break from the healing work—a concept that took me a while to accept. The idea that it's okay to hit pause. Not quit, not abandon yourself, but pause long enough to integrate.

Growth doesn't move in a straight line. It's progress, plateau, progress. And when you're in a plateau, it's easy to believe you're losing ground. You're not. You don't go back to who you were before. That version of you doesn't exist anymore. You've shifted reality. You've moved time. Even if you pause, you're not the same person when you resume; you're a new person continuing.

Before you start this healing path, you will likely encounter some mental roadblocks. Your mind will tell you that you don't have the time. Your mind will tell you that you're too old or that it's too late. Your mind will tell you that you're too busy, too sick, or too far gone.

You have to stop negotiating with the voice that is your mind.

The body might whisper before shouts. But if you keep ignoring it like your mind keeps telling you to, the whispers become shouts, and then the shouts become screams.

CHAPTER TEN

Trauma as a Doorway Back to the Soul

It wasn't until my first soul retrieval that I finally realized trauma isn't just pain but a doorway back to my soul.

When I went into my first soul retrieval, as a participant, I wanted to go in without any preconceived notions or expectations about what would happen. I didn't want to be influenced by other people's stories or walk into it trying to "match" an experience. I wanted whatever happened to be *mine.* I was very intentional about staying as neutral as possible.

The session started in a way that felt deceptively normal: conversation. Simple questions. What's been happening in your life? What's happening in your body? What's showing up right now? What has happened in your past?

At the time, I thought we were just talking. Now I understand that something different was happening: I was being given an opening for truth to surface. An opening for the parts of me I had compartmentalized to finally speak.

The things that came out of my mouth surprised me. Not because they were untrue, but because I could feel how much I had stored away, filed under "handled" or "not relevant anymore."

I talked about grief I didn't realize was still living in me. Experiences I could describe intellectually but had never fully metabolized. Pieces of my past that were easy to summarize and hard to feel. Family patterns. Addiction. Instability. Survival.

Then the shaman said, "Okay. Now we begin."

Her style was vocal and demonstrative. She narrated what she was perceiving as she went, almost as if she was tracking a landscape out loud. It was like we crossed a threshold from talking about my life to touching something underneath it. I could feel the transformation.

Here's what struck me the most: She wasn't repeating my story back to me. She was speaking directly to the parts of the story I couldn't fully verbalize, the parts beneath the surface. She described the energetic "why" behind certain moments. The soul-level impact. The ways a person's spirit can step back or fragment, not because it's weak, but because it's protecting itself. She spoke about the internal cost of events I had treated like they were just... life.

Over several hours, I started connecting dots I didn't even know were separated. It wasn't just that I had trauma. I had learned to survive by dividing myself. I'd survived by isolating experiences, emotions, memories, and parts of my identity so I could keep functioning.

Then something happened that became a turning point for me: She described seeing an intense, almost overwhelming energetic "attachment" that didn't make sense to her at first, something layered, repetitive, and deeply embedded. As she worked to clear it, she realized she needed additional help. Shamans often work with a team of "guides" from the spirit world. These guides can take the form of power animals, human ancestors, saints, or spiritual higher beings.

While she was working, I had a shift, an immediate internal knowing. This wasn't a thought I had to reason through. It was a recognition that landed in my body: *This isn't only mine.* That's the best way I can say it.

That's when I realized that in certain environments where you witness or absorb a lot of human suffering, other people's trauma can cling to you. Not as a metaphor, but an actual energetic residue. A burden you carry without understanding why you feel so heavy, why you're so exhausted, why your nervous system can't come back down.

This realization connected to something another practitioner said to me earlier, about the feeling of being "painfully blocked" in a way that wasn't just stress, as if something was lodged in my system and couldn't move. That it was like "having a thousand screams trapped in your throat." She even recommended that I go somewhere that I felt safe and just let myself scream, make noise, get the sound out. At the time, I didn't understand it. I thought, *"I speak up. I'm not silenced. I'm not afraid to tell the truth."*

After that soul retrieval, I understood. You can be outspoken and still carry suppression in your body. You can be "strong" and still be holding thousands of moments you never gave yourself permission to release.

That session flipped a switch.

Suddenly the story wasn't, "Here are the traumatic things that happened to me." The story became, "Here is what those things did to my energy, my body, my nervous system, my sense of self, and my capacity to stay connected."

It then widened even more. I saw how much of what we experience individually is not isolated. It's collective. It's layered. It's inherited. It's absorbed. It's normalized. A lot of it never gets healed, so it keeps circulating through bodies, families, institutions, relationships, and communities.

That session was the moment trauma stopped being "just trauma" for me. Trauma became a doorway: the door that forced me to see what I had been carrying and that gave me a path back to myself.

The Empathic Soul: When Sensitivity Becomes Trauma

Empathy is not a flaw, but being an empath is a "power" that needs protection. As I mentioned before, if an empath is operating unprotected, it can become a form of trauma.

From my understanding and my own living knowledge, empathy at this level originates at the soul level. It isn't something you decide to become. It isn't a personality trait you pick up along the way. It's something you arrive with.

I see being an empath as a reflection of a soul that has already done a certain amount of clearing or integration in other lifetimes. There's a clarity there, a thinner layer between pure consciousness and the human experience. The empath has that "cleaner pane of glass" we talked about earlier.

Because of that clarity, an empath can feel what others are feeling. Sometimes emotionally, sometimes physically, sometimes intuitively, without needing words or explanation. Some people call this empathy. Some call it highly intuitive. Some call it psychic sensitivity. To me, they're all expressions of the same thing. And it is a gift.

The problem isn't the gift. The problem is that no one hands you a user manual. You don't come into this life knowing how to manage that sensitivity. You don't come in knowing how to differentiate what's yours to feel from what isn't. You don't automatically know how to stay open without being overwhelmed. Instead, you enter the world exposed.

If you're deeply empathic, you feel everything: other people's emotions, other people's stress, other people's pain. Sometimes before they even know they're feeling it themselves.

Until you learn otherwise, you assume it's all *you*. You think you're anxious, depressed, angry, or unstable. When in reality, you may be absorbing the emotional field around you. And that emotional field is *all* around you.

Some people walk into a room and bring calm. Others bring chaos. Some people unconsciously pull energy from others because they don't know how to regulate themselves. If you're empathic and unprotected, you feel all of it. And you feel it intensely.

Without the right tools, boundaries, and awareness, this becomes destabilizing. You're constantly shifting, responding, and adjusting to everyone else's internal state. Over time, that creates exhaustion, confusion, and eventually trauma, not from a single event, but from prolonged energetic overload.

Another layer of this is exposure.

We are energetic beings. Any form of interaction—physical, emotional, even digital—creates some level of energetic exchange. If you don't know how to recognize this and disengage from it, you end up carrying connections that drain you long after the interaction is over.

Again, this isn't because something is "wrong" with you. It's because no one taught you how to protect yourself. Being an empath isn't traumatic by nature, but being an empath without awareness, boundaries, or integration can absolutely cause trauma. When that goes unrecognized for years (or decades), it compounds just like any other form of unprocessed trauma.

That's why empathy, when misunderstood, can feel like a burden instead of a gift. Learning how to work *with* it, rather than being consumed by it, is essential to healing, embodiment, and staying whole in this human experience.

Early Imprints, the Soul's Blueprint, and Choice

For anyone reading this book, if you think your sensitivity began early in life, this is important. If much of our subconscious wiring forms in the first years of childhood, how does that interact with the soul's nature? For people who come into this life highly sensitive or empathic: How much of that early exposure shapes trauma later on? And how does that compare to what happens in adulthood?

The question underneath it all: Is trauma part of the soul's design?

This is where things can feel controversial; people often hear this idea as having no choice in life. Or as if life was predisposed and there's nothing they can do about the way things are. That's not how I understand it.

From my perspective, the soul enters this life already aware of the terrain it's stepping into. It knows the family system, the environment, the emotional themes, and the potential challenges it may face. Not in a rigid, predetermined way, but more like a loose blueprint.

The soul carries immense awareness, far more than the typical conscious human mind has access to. It knows the lessons available, the possible paths, and the range of choices that could unfold across a lifetime. But knowing the terrain doesn't mean the journey is fixed.

Choice exists, constantly.

There are certain major points of growth that will eventually be encountered in the soul's evolution. Whether those moments are met in this lifetime or another is up to the choices made along the way. Nothing is forced. Nothing is locked in. There is design, but it is *flexible and adaptable.*

In the early years of life, a child's soul is already responding. Even before conscious reasoning develops, the soul is adapting, deciding how to relate to what it encounters. That's why two children raised in the same environment can grow into completely different adults. Their experiences may look similar on the surface, but the internal responses, the meaning made, the role assumed, and the coping strategies formed are different.

For empathic or highly sensitive children, this early period can be especially impactful. They may be absorbing far more than they understand. Without guidance, protection, or language for what they're feeling, those impressions can take root deeply.

But none of that is permanent.

Even if certain patterns are established early, they are not unchangeable. The soul always retains agency. At any point in life, a different choice can be made. A new direction can be chosen. That's why we see people radically transform, sometimes after decades of living one way.

Growth doesn't disappear just because it's delayed. If someone steps away from inner work in this lifetime, it doesn't mean they've failed. It simply means they pause where they are. The learning continues when they're ready, whether that is now or later. The soul doesn't move backward. It builds.

Even when lessons repeat, they do so with greater awareness and capacity each time. Trauma isn't punishment. It isn't a flaw in the design. And it isn't proof that something went wrong. Trauma is one of the ways the soul encounters itself through the human experience. How, and when, that encounter unfolds remains a choice.

Spiritual Practice as the Bridge Between Trauma and the Soul

Before going into how spiritual practices, of any kind, help bridge the gap between pain, trauma, healing, and reconnection to the soul, I want to make a distinction between *ritual* and *practice.*

Ritual, whether religious or spiritual, exists to humble us. It's meant to remind us that there is something greater than the individual self. That we can release control, surrender effort, and remember we are not alone.

Ritual creates a container. But ritual without devotion leaves the container empty.

You can repeat prayers, light candles, burn incense, attend services, or follow routines endlessly. But if those actions aren't paired with sincerity, faith, and presence, they become mechanical. At that point, it's just movement. The only ones who know your intentions are you and whatever higher truth you believe in.

Practice is similar. You can meditate, do yoga, chant, or engage in any discipline simply because you think you're *supposed* to. But when practice is done only out of obligation, without intention or surrender, it doesn't transform anything. It becomes another task.

What changes everything is submission. Not submission as weakness, but as trust.

When practice is combined with genuine devotion, when you enter it with the willingness to let go of control, that's when something opens. That opening is what allows connection to form.

It doesn't matter which tradition you follow. Stillness can come through prayer, meditation, chanting, singing, movement, breath, or silence. The form doesn't matter nearly as much as the sincerity behind it. When you fully engage, when the noise quiets and the ego loosens, you create space for healing.

Trauma can't fully heal in constant noise.We may cope. We may manage symptoms. But deep healing requires moments where the mind softens enough for the soul to be felt. Spiritual practices create these moments by allowing the nervous system to settle and the deeper self to emerge. This space is also where forgiveness enters, not just forgiveness of others but of ourselves. Many people want the relief that forgiveness brings, yet forget that they deserve that same grace.

Healing requires acknowledging our humanity; we survived the best way we knew how, with the tools we had at the time.

Trauma, the Human, and the Soul in Daily Life

When asked how trauma, the human experience, and the soul can be integrated into everyday life, there's no easy, right, or wrong answer.

The truth is: Complete integration is a lifelong process.

Total integration would imply full enlightenment, and that's not something a person simply decides to achieve overnight. Growth unfolds gradually. Each human is a work in progress. Integration begins with clarity.

First, define what growth or self-realization means *to you*. This belongs to you, and only you. Growth and self-realization should not be based on what others say they should look like, but on what alignment, peace, and integrity mean in your own life.

Second, explore the question: *Who am I?* Not as a role, a profession, or a personality, but what's beneath those layers. Who are you when labels fall away? This inquiry takes time, patience, and self-reflection.

Once you begin to understand those two things, compassion for yourself and your healing path naturally follows. You stop demanding perfection from yourself. You learn to forgive missteps in your development without abandoning accountability. And you fully open up to the healing process.

From there, integration becomes practical. It shows up in everyday moments, in how you speak, in how you respond, and in how you treat yourself and others. In each situation, you can ask: *Am I acting in alignment with who I am?* If the answer is no, you still have power. Every moment offers a new choice. This path does require effort. It asks for honesty. It asks you to notice when you're acting out of fear instead of truth or habit instead of intention. The reward is authenticity, living in a way that feels whole.

Integration is about presence. It's about choosing alignment, again and again, even when it's difficult. This is how trauma becomes not just something you survived, but something that guides you back to yourself.

Healing, Hope, and the Meaning of the Work

How do you know the healing work is actually working? You feel calmer.

Not euphoric.

Not fixed.

Just calmer, clearer, more present.

Then you start responding differently. You pause. You notice yourself choosing how you want to show up instead of reacting the way you always have. Other people notice it too. They may not be able to name it, but they feel it.

You still get triggered.

You still feel anger.

You still feel frustration.

You are still human.But there's a moment, sometimes just a second, where you realize: *This isn't about others. This is about who I want to be.* That awareness alone is a sign the work is doing something. Then there are the physical signs. They're usually subtle at first: a slower resting heart rate, better sleep, clearer skin, fewer cravings driven by a need for emotional regulation, and a body that feels less "on edge."

Healing arrives as small changes that add up. After feeling those subtle changes and being aware of my progress, one of the biggest shifts for me was looking in the mirror. Not to judge. Not to criticize. To really look into my own eyes. For the first time, I did not see anger or exhaustion, or someone bracing for what's next, or something I didn't like. This time, I saw *peace*.

That's when I knew something real had changed.

A Moment of Healing That Called for a Pause

During our interview for this section, I noticed Gina was struggling. We paused. As two women navigating different healing journeys, we knew this pause was needed. We knew this was a message. Her struggle brought up a beautiful opportunity to explore self-acceptance and self-love. To perhaps create a shift for her and to consider how her trauma could be a doorway back to a deeper soul connection.

This was a chance to "keep clearing the glass."

With a choked throat and fighting teary eyes, Gina shared, "This hits really hard. When I look in the mirror, I don't always like what I see, who I see. I think, I know, part of my work, maybe even my purpose, is to learn how to truly love myself. Not intellectually. Not someday. But here. Now. As imperfect as I am, today. Love myself to self-forgive. It's in that forgiveness that I will know I'm progressing in my journey. But it is so hard.

I'm sharing this to show you that you're not alone. Like my ghostwriter and friend, many of us struggle with these feelings. If this moment of healing resonates with you, know that it's ok if this process feels hard. Full and complete self-acceptance, self-forgiveness, and true self-love doesn't always come easy. That struggle can feel like you're not progressing or as if you're going backward.

You're not going backward. You're changed. Even when it doesn't feel like it. The person you were before doesn't exist anymore. The mere awareness of it all is a clear sign of the work you've done. What's happening is that your mind is fighting to stay in control. It always does. It's done that "control thing" your entire life.

When you start stepping into something deeper, something truer, the mind panics. It brings up old voices. Old stories. Old wounds. Your mind wants the familiar. But your *SOUL* chose this life. It chose *YOU*, knowing everything about *YOU*. Your soul didn't choose you because you were perfect. It chose you because you were *capable*. Capable of learning. Capable of healing. Capable of becoming something more.

No one will ever love you the way your soul loves you. Not a parent. Not a partner. Not anyone. That love existed before you ever took a breath in this life. So, when those brutal inner voices show up, the ones you would never allow anyone to say to someone you love, you get to tell them NO! You will not be able to silence them forever. You just need to remember that *they are not the truth.*

If you are still deep in the trenches of trauma, deep in its hold, I want you to know two things:

First, what doesn't kill you really can make you stronger, but only if you let yourself heal. Healing requires tending the wound instead of ignoring it. Pretending something didn't happen or "pushing through" is not healing. A healed bone is stronger where it once broke. The same is true for the soul connection.

Second, *t*his too shall pass. I'm not saying this in a dismissive or toxic "just be positive" way. This too shall pass in a soul-level way. If something has an ending, it isn't the whole truth of who you are. It's an experience, not your identity. This doesn't mean it didn't matter. It means it doesn't define you forever.

You, your soul, your truth—it has no ending. It's infinite; you just have to keep "clearing the glass."

The real meaning of hope and faith for me is knowing that my soul chose this life. What I came here to do, I already carry. I don't need to rush. I don't need to prove anything. I just need to keep taking the next step.

As for the world... We're waking up.

Most people are questioning. Most people are seeking. Most people are choosing healing instead of avoidance. We're part of something bigger than we realize. Each person who chooses to heal changes more than just themselves.

That's where my hope, my faith, lives today.

Before You Go On

If you feel tired after reading Part III, it's normal, expected even. It's a signal. Part III was not meant to be consumed quickly or "understood" all at once. Much of what you just read is not information for the mind; it's recognition for the body and memory for the soul. That kind of learning settles slowly.

After reading Part III, you are not expected to feel healed, resolved, inspired, or even hopeful. You are only invited to notice. Notice how your body feels as you pause here. Notice your breath. Notice whether something softened, even slightly, or whether something feels tender and exposed.

As mentioned before, healing is not a straight line. It is not proven by some dramatic change. Often, the earliest sign that something is shifting is simply awareness without judgment. The moment you can witness your experience instead of fighting it, fixing it, or explaining it away, an important shift has begun.

If nothing feels different, that does not mean that nothing is happening. Some truths arrive quietly. Some land later. And some wait until you feel safe enough to receive them.

You do not need to do anything with what you've read. You do not need to analyze your trauma, define your soul, or map out your next steps. There is no assignment here. There is no expectation that you "apply" this work perfectly.

Let this chapter rest inside you.

If it stirred something, trust that your system knows how to carry it forward in its own time and in its own way. If it didn't stir something, trust that too. Not every door opens the moment we touch it.

Before continuing, consider giving yourself a few quiet moments. No phone. No distraction. Just stillness. Even a minute is enough.

And remember this:

You are not behind.

You are not broken.

You are not doing this wrong.

You are human. And, you are learning how to listen again.

CHAPTER ELEVEN

The Realization

There was an edge I couldn't quite get over, a realization that I circled around before it fully landed. I remember saying to myself: *I need to go deeper. I need to be more raw. I need to push a little further.* I could feel a big shift coming, a transformation, a remembering of what is true. It was during one of many deep conversations with my two best friends that I finally said it out loud, "I wasn't broken."

I had learned to lean heavily into one part of myself and had neglected another. I embraced my masculine side—the strength, the toughness, the enforcer, the doer—and completely pushed aside the softer, more feminine parts of myself. The gentle parts. The vulnerable parts. At the time, that's what I needed to do to survive.

I remember describing it like that Japanese art, Kintsugi, where broken pottery is repaired with gold. It wasn't that I was shattered. I was sealing myself back together in a way that made me more whole and more beautiful, not damaged.

That was the first crack in breaking the belief that I wasn't broken.

The realization solidified further during a healing session with my friend and Shamanic Practitioner, Michelle Taylor, from Wellness Rising Within. Like me, Michelle's work and her gifts lie in many modalities. This session was part meditation, part regression, part hypnosis. The kind of work where boundaries blur and the body and subconscious speak to each other.

Michelle asked me to go to a time when I felt whole.

And I couldn't.

I searched backward through my life and realized there was no memory where I felt fully whole. That realization alone broke me open. I cried with my eyes closed, realizing I had always believed that I was damaged in some way.

Then she said something that stuck with me: "Sometimes you have to go forward." She asked me to move forward in time, to meet a version of myself who was whole.

As I went through this exercise, I saw what I understood to be my true self—an older version of me in this lifetime. She was dressed in white, soft and feminine, grounded and calm. Not distant or untouchable. Just... Me. All of me.

Then Michelle asked me to merge with that version of me.

What came next was simple and overwhelming: I wasn't, at that time, energetically too far off from that true, whole version of me.

Don't get me wrong, I still had a lot to learn, uncover, and heal, but the core of who that whole and healed version of me was felt very close and attainable from where the core of me was in the moment. The overwhelmingly profound realization came over me like lava rushing from a volcano;

if a future version of me was whole, then the current version of me wasn't broken.

What I felt next was an intense, unconditional love. A kind of love that's hard to describe. This was deeper than parental love, deeper than acceptance. It was the kind of love that I have only ever felt during meditation or when in the presence of my beloved Guruji and the swamis that I have been blessed enough to spend time learning from.

It was self-recognition: *Of course you're here. Of course you belong.*

That's when it fully landed. Who I was, *who I am*, wasn't wrong. I was already on the path. I was already close. I didn't need fixing. What was missing was learning how to love myself. Your true self isn't separate from you; it's who you are in your most authentic expression in this lifetime or in any lifetime.

It's not hard to see how it can all feel like "you" are multiple layers: the ego-self navigating daily life, the true self waiting to be embodied, and the higher consciousness beyond both.

Forgiveness is the Bridge

Struggling between *feeling broken* and *remembering wholeness* is part of the process. It's also a sign that you are moving through the layers of self. For me, the biggest difference came down to forgiveness, especially of oneself.

I went through a phase where I believed that becoming my "true self" meant becoming endlessly loving, kind, and free of anger or resentment. *If this higher version of me exists, then I must have to get rid of everything dark inside me first.*

I started asking myself:

Do I need to forgive every person who's ever hurt me?

Do I need to cut cords with everyone I feel resentment toward?

Do I need to clean up every past wound before I'm allowed to be whole?

Having already experienced the love that comes with remembering wholeness, my commitment to this journey wasn't wavering. I kept doing the work: asking the hard questions, staying compassionate with myself, and being intentional with practices. I've already mentioned that forgiving my soul was the hardest work I've done in this journey. What I eventually understood, though, was that the most important person I needed to forgive was myself. Deep, unconditional forgiveness is the bridge to remembering wholeness. I needed to forgive myself for agreeing to this life.

For the choices I made.

For the situations I stayed in.

For the ways I survived.

The truth is, I don't have control over what other people do. I never did. But I *did* carry judgment, blame, and anger toward myself for being there at all. You can't fully access love while holding resentment. You can't embody compassion while carrying self-hatred. And you can't remember who you truly are if you're still punishing yourself for surviving. Remembering wholeness, for me, was about releasing the belief that I had failed myself. Until you learn how to truly forgive yourself, wholeness will always feel just out of reach.

Wholeness does not mean you never feel anger, grief, or frustration again. It means you no longer live inside the emotions. Remember, every emotion is meant to move through us, not take up residence. Much like what we're made of, neutrons, protons, and electrons are always moving. We must let energy, including emotions, continue to move. If there's ever a place to be radically honest, it's here. You must learn to honestly sit with how you speak to yourself, judge yourself, and how you relate to your own story. Only then will you be able to see yourself as the infinite light you are. The difference between *feeling broken* and *remembering wholeness* isn't that your life suddenly looks different. It's that you stop seeing yourself as something that needs to be fixed.

What about love?

Is love an emotion? A deep emotion that transcends feelings? Or is it something else? Ask around, and you'll get different answers. Search dictionaries and platforms, and you'll find a bunch of different definitions and even contradictions. But there is an intersection between human love and divine love. When asked to expand on love, my response is, "I see human love, and I see divine love."

The love we experience as humans is deep, meaningful, and very real to us, but still shaped by conditions, roles, expectations, and endings. Human love is conditional, even when we don't want to admit it. Take the love we have for our children. We call it unconditional, but there are still expectations woven into it: that they grow, that they respect us, that they survive, that they don't completely destroy themselves or us in the process. This doesn't make human love wrong, or less real. It just makes it, well, *human*.

Human love exists within its current lifetime and has a beginning and an end.

Divine love is different. Divine love doesn't have a beginning or an end; it doesn't end when a relationship changes or a life cycle closes. It isn't dependent on behavior and doesn't break when someone disappoints you.

Divine love says, "I see you, a being made of the same source as me. You exist, and because of that, I love you."

Divine love has no conditions and no expectations. It's not emotional in the way we usually think of emotion. It's experiential. It's a state of being. It loves you because you exist.

But divine love doesn't mean tolerating harmful behavior or staying in unsafe situations. Boundaries and discernment still exist. Divine love means you no longer need hatred or resentment to justify your boundaries. You can see someone's humanity, struggles, and wounds without allowing them to harm you.

For most of us, knowing the difference in human love and divine love isn't something we wake up just understanding one day. It's learned. Slowly. Through experience, through practice, and most of all, through forgiveness.

Divine love is a love that simply *is*. This is the love remembered as we come back into alignment with our true self.

CHAPTER TWELVE

Practices That Help You Remember Wholeness

THE 3 PATHS

Kriya as a Path of Listening

At its heart, Kriya is an ancient meditative tradition. Different lineages trace it back through generations of teachers and students, master to disciple, disciple to the next disciple. There are some theoretical and physical variations across lineages, but the intention is universal: communication with the Divine while learning to work with your energy and awareness in a grounded way.

I addressed this briefly earlier in the context of my experience, but if I may, I'd love to address this head-on from a broader perspective.

As I mentioned in Part II, to learn the practice of Kriya Yoga, you have to go through initiation. If your mind immediately goes to: *Is this a cult? Why is it secret? Why can't someone just tell me the steps? What about this lineage?* I get it. Coming from a Western and Christian framework, I had the same initial reaction. Here, I'm going deeper as to why this teaching piece is so important.

From my perspective, one of the reasons it's guarded is responsibility. Deep meditation can change you—your nervous system, your habits, your perception, your sense of identity. Modern science supports the idea that intensive meditation corresponds with measurable changes in the brain. You don't need to "believe" anything mystical to respect that real physiological changes happen when someone practices meditation deeply and consistently. Without guidance, it can feel overwhelming. People can push too hard and destabilize themselves. A teacher helps you slow down, integrate, and stay steady.

Speaking in generalities, in that lineage structure, "Initiation" is better understood as "teaching." It's typically a weekend (or a focused period) where you learn the practice, ask questions, and practice with guidance. Depending on the specific tradition, you may receive energetic support, cleansing, and balance as part of the process. It's immersive in the sense that you're in an environment shaped by meditation and prayer. It's like being in the woods. People naturally get quieter. Things settle.

In plain terms, without going into specifics, Kriya is a structured and scientific process that is a combination of breathwork and spinal manipulation (posture) designed to support the nervous system, open the body, and help energy flow more freely. All while slowing the breath rate and turning the focus toward divinity. The breath patterns are intentional. It's no secret we live in a constant low-grade stress state without realizing it. Breath is one of the most direct ways to influence that.

During the teaching, there's an aspect of learning to work with your attention and energy with more intention. Not to force anything. That's not the point. It's learning to just practice and surrender without attachment.

Everyone's experience will be different. Your meditation won't feel like mine. What people often notice is a growing sense of calm, clarity, and steadiness. Longer meditations can feel like a celebration. Not because you "achieved" a time limit, but because that longer period of true quiet can bring a kind of peace that's hard to describe until you feel it.

There's also something reassuring about entering a tradition that's well respected, where people guiding you aren't trying to "get" something from you. Some of the most humbling, loving interactions I've experienced have been within the Kriya community—from teachers, senior practitioners, and people doing simple service work. There isn't a "pay more, access more" vibe. There's no such thing as an "all-access pass" to holiness.

If this type of tradition piqued your curiosity, a good place to start can be Kriya Yoga International. They have ashrams and meditation centers in multiple areas across the world. Their site lists locations by region. It's a practical starting point if someone wants structure and a real lineage container.

Nature as Your Path to Reconnection

Nature not only reminds you of wholeness, but it actually helps you integrate back into it. Nature shows up in healing. Nature will help confirm that a state of healing is taking place. Nature, especially plants and minerals, is pure energy. There's no malice there. There's intelligence, but it's collective rather than personal. Each element vibrates at its own frequency and contributes to the whole.

This isn't just metaphysical language; it's observable. Trees support entire ecosystems by taking nutrients and giving oxygen.. Birds, soil, roots, minerals—everything is interconnected and exchanging energy constantly. That interconnectedness is very close to our true nature.

When you haven't experienced direct connection with your higher consciousness, nature is often the closest doorway. It's a living reminder of what it feels like to be part of something whole. Humans have very effectively built lives that keep us boxed away from nature. Our minds tell us we're separate from it, but we aren't. We're made of the same elements. That separation itself becomes a kind of trauma. When we cut ourselves off from the natural exchange of energy that our bodies and souls need, something goes dormant.

Reconnection is the healing.

At a certain level of spiritual development, someone may not need to physically sit with a tree to feel that connection; they can access it internally. Most of us aren't there yet. We need the experience. Just like I wear white to remind myself that softness, femininity, and gentleness are allowed, being in nature reminds us that we belong. That we are not outside of life, but within it.

Our bodies need oxygen. They need water. They need sunlight. But beyond that, they need the energy of the natural world. As my friend Gina would say, "We're basically plants with complicated emotions."

One of my favorite practices is to simply SIT in nature. No agenda. No destination. Just listening and waiting. Nature always gives you what you need. Sometimes it's a bird going about its ordinary life. Sometimes it's the quiet presence of a tree. Sometimes it's an animal crossing your path or the feeling of wind. In the stillness, nature speaks.

We tend to make everything goal-oriented. Even hiking becomes about miles and endpoints. When you let stillness be the destination, when you let yourself just sit, your body responds. Your breathing slows. Your heart rate drops. Your shoulders soften. That physiological shift is part of wholeness returning.

If there's a tree that draws you (most people have one), pay attention. Trees have distinct qualities, just like animals. Birch carries calm and coolness. Aspen carries movement and lightness. When you sit with a tree and allow yourself to receive what it offers, something in you mirrors that quality.

It's another way we reconnect to divinity, not as something distant, but as something living, breathing, and present. The connection is already there. It's just a matter of choosing to return to it. Even five minutes outside can start that process.

The trauma is the disconnection.

The healing is the reconnection.

Shamanism as a Path to Remembering

My draw to nature-based and Earth-based faith systems has always been strong. While Kriya is part of my personal practice and my spiritual anchor, shamanism, for me, started as a *"remembering."* Before Kriya, I studied multiple religions and spiritual traditions, from Biblical studies to a two-year program in the upper and lower fundamentals of Buddhism to the psychology of Buddhism. I now study a combination of the Bible, Vedic texts, and Hinduism with shamanism thrown in to keep things interesting.

The last area I explored personally before everything shifted was an intense and immersive study of Paganism and Wiccan traditions. My interest stemmed from being deeply drawn to nature and Earth-based traditions. Systems that acknowledge divinity in all beings: plants, animals, and humans. Systems that understand energy as something we interact with, not something abstract.

As mentioned earlier, when I began my Kriya practice, one of the things I did early on was keep a notebook. Before each meditation, I would write down a question. I wasn't meditating *on* the question—I just wrote it down so it was anchored in my awareness. Then I would meditate. When I finished, I would write again. While my mind was still connected to that heightened conscious state, the answers would come through freely, like a channeling, but instead of an external entity, it was a connection to my highest self.

When the question of "purpose" came up, what came through was soul healer. This is when shamanism came back into my life in a more formal manner.

At the time, having the term "soul healer" come through my meditation felt deeply unhelpful. I had no idea what that meant. I didn't even know that "soul healer" was a thing. As we discussed earlier, I started digging and found that soul healing came from shamanism. Soul healing. Soul retrieval. Practices that work not just with the mind and body, but with the energetic and spiritual wounds people carry, often beneath conscious awareness.

Suddenly, things started to connect: trauma, fragmentation, the sense of not being whole. In those days, I was starting to experience soul retrieval work. I can't say for certain which came first, but these occurrences were happening in the same season of my life. That's when I realized this wasn't about adopting a new belief system. It was about remembering a way of working that already existed within me and learning how to do it safely.

Like most people, I thought shamanism was something you were born into, within a specific community of elders who learned from generations ago. I didn't know there were teachers, lineages, or structured ways to learn these practices responsibly. I didn't know that becoming a shamanic practitioner was even an option. But I could not ignore this calling, so I researched: How does this work? Who teaches this? Is mentorship involved? How do you learn without opening yourself up to things you don't understand?

My research led me to the work of Sandra Ingerman and Michael Harner, and through them, to Core Shamanism. From there, I found a long-practicing shamanic practitioner named Michelle McKinney from Northwest Healing and Intuitive Arts, who had been trained and certified to teach these methods. She offered structured classes rooted in lineage and ethics, which mattered to me, deeply.

By that point, I knew I was energetically sensitive, what I call "an energetic magnet," while also having what I call "wandering energy." If there is a wounded energy nearby, my energy just takes a mosey on over to offer it a hug. My instinct has always been to open, to heal, and to connect. But not all energy is benevolent. Not all spaces are safe. I didn't want to approach this work naïvely or romantically. I wanted containment. I wanted guidance. I wanted to understand how to navigate these realms responsibly, both for myself and for others.

Shamanism didn't enter my life as something exotic, trendy, or supernatural. It entered as the missing language for something I already knew was true: *H*ealing doesn't stop at the mind or the body, and wholeness often requires retrieving parts of ourselves we didn't even realize were missing. The choice to study shamanism was about learning how to do the work consciously, ethically, and with humility. It didn't begin as a career decision. It began as a *remembering*.

CHAPTER THIRTEEN

Shamanism: A Deeper Look

What Shamanism Means to Me

During our interview, Gina asked, "What does shamanism mean to you? Not the dictionary definition, not how it's often portrayed. What does it mean personally, now that you've studied it and lived it?" Shamanism begins with one essential truth: a shaman is someone who has healed themselves.

That understanding comes from early anthropological research, long before modern spirituality reframed the term. Across cultures and continents, shamans were often individuals who had undergone profound personal suffering and healing. Sometimes they were chosen by lineage, sometimes selected by another shaman, sometimes called through illness or crisis. They were trained and mentored, not self-appointed.

They were also protected by their communities. Their insight and healing ability were seen as vital to the health of the whole tribe. Because of that, they often lived somewhat apart—revered, guarded, and respected.

That foundation is important.

In modern practice, in what's known as Core Shamanism, the work has become more global and less tribal, while still preserving essential principles. Core Shamanism identifies practices that appear across cultures: soul retrieval, power animal retrieval, depossession, and psychopomp work. All are methods that address fragmentation of the soul and disruptions in a person's energetic system.

At the heart of Core Shamanism, the shaman's role is to help restore what has been lost or displaced.

Some shamans work primarily with plant medicine. Others with minerals, water, or elemental forces. Some are drawn to animal energy, some to earth-based healing. While many practitioners can work across these realms, most develop affinities. Mine is very clearly animal-based and earth-based.

The practices themselves are consistent. Soul retrieval addresses places where trauma has caused parts of the self to disconnect. Depossession works with energies that don't belong to the person. Psychopomp work helps spirits who are earthbound to move on. In that sense, shamans have always functioned much like priests or spiritual guides, tending not just to the living but to the unseen.

Where my perspective deepened was through studying shamanism alongside yogic philosophy. As I studied both, I began to see something unmistakable: These traditions are speaking the same language, using different symbols.

Early yogic practice, long before organized Hinduism, was shamanic in nature. This isn't unique to India. Every continent and every ancient culture developed similar systems. Which raises an important question: How do vastly different cultures arrive at the same core truths?

My understanding is this: Trauma doesn't block the soul; it clouds access to it.

The soul is always present. What trauma does is dirty the glass between our conscious mind and our deeper knowing. Ego, fear, conditioning, and lived experience layer over that connection. The shaman doesn't *give* someone their soul back. The person must seek the healing themselves. The shaman simply helps guide them in connecting how to clear part of the glass, enough for light to come through again.

That's why this work has existed for thousands of years.

From that lens, power animal retrieval and connection to spirit guides, deities, or directions are not separate acts. They are different pathways to the same source. If divinity exists in all things, then connecting with an animal spirit, a deity, or the land itself is simply another way of connecting with that divine energy.

There is no wrong way for divinity to reveal itself to someone.

These forms exist because the human mind needs structure. Pure unity is overwhelming. Symbols allow us to relate.

Ancestry, Integrity, and Respect

Having traced shamanic roots within my own ancestry, I was hesitant about how I should approach this work. At first, I was deeply concerned about appropriation. I didn't want to study or practice within a cultural tradition that I had no right to. I didn't want to take something sacred from another lineage and claim it as my own. That mattered to me.

When I first did DNA testing, I learned that while I wasn't as much Native as I had assumed, there *were* tribal medicine people in my lineage, far back, but present. Then the same thing appeared in my Portuguese ancestry. Then German. And especially Irish and Scottish. What surprised me most wasn't the ancestry itself; it was recognizing practices I was already doing instinctively.

At one point, I explained a grounding technique to someone, and they said, "That's really complicated. You don't need to do all that." But I *knew* I needed to. Later, I discovered that the technique was Druidic, Celtic in origin. I hadn't learned it anywhere. It came through me.

That was the knowing.

I eventually understood that these practices don't belong to cultures. They belong to the soul. Culture gives them language, and lineage gives them form. But divinity itself isn't owned. When people say, "You can't access this because it's mine," that's ego, not spirit.

Respect and humility are essential. But divinity is not proprietary. If you approach the practice with the highest level of respect and from a place that has pure intent and you're not claiming to own or have created something God-given, then you're not appropriating; you're practicing as God intended.

This realization was reinforced through Kriya, which is non-sectarian. People from all faiths practice together. No one claims ownership. The emphasis is on faithful practice, devotion, humility, and divine love, not identity. If all of this is pointing to the same truth, then no one is excluded. The differences exist so that each person can access the divine in a way their nervous system can handle.

Understanding this allowed me to step into this work not as someone taking something that isn't hers, but as someone remembering what has always been available.

A Homecoming to the Soul

A lot of practitioners keep their power animals private, and that's completely valid. I have energetic beings, what I call "my council," who've made it very clear that they don't want to be named or discussed publicly. I respect that.

When I was fifteen, without knowing what it was, I went on what I now understand was a vision quest. I had no guidance, no framework, and no understanding of the practice. I simply decided I was going to fast for three days, meditate, and find my spirit animal as a rite of passage. Fifteen-year-old me thought this was perfectly reasonable. Looking back, I realize how unusual that was.

During that quest, I connected with a wolf. She's been with me ever since, though I didn't always know it. Years later, I tattooed her on my shoulder, right around the time I became pregnant with my daughter. I wanted a permanent reminder that she was always there.

And then... I forgot.

Life happened. Marriage. Divorce. Children. Another marriage. A career in law enforcement. And eventually, my conversion to Christianity. Somewhere along the way, I decided I couldn't have that connection anymore. I believed it wasn't allowed. So I stopped listening. I stopped feeling her presence.

Years passed.

When I eventually went through my formal power animal retrieval, our teacher said something simple but powerful: "You might think you know who your animal is, but don't force it. Just let the journey unfold."

At that point, I hadn't felt my wolf in close to twenty years. During the ceremony, she was there... waiting. My first thought was not astonishment. It was grief. *Where did you go?*

Her response was immediate and clear: *I never left. You just stopped listening.*

That moment gutted me.. Because it was true.

The beauty of that experience wasn't about discovering something new. It was about remembering something ancient and deeply familiar. I didn't yet understand divinity the way I do now. I didn't see her as an expression of God or Consciousness or Energy. I just felt the connection, and that was enough—a true homecoming to the soul.

Since that day, there hasn't been a single day I haven't meditated and connected with her. Not one.

That journey of reconnecting with my power animal stands apart from others I've done, even the ones I facilitate for other people. When I journey for someone else, especially during a power animal retrieval, I don't bring something back *for* them. I take them *with* me. I want them to experience the connection themselves, to know they have that ability.

I've seen how powerful it is when someone realizes they don't need an intermediary to access a part of their own divinity. And to this day, nothing quite compares to that moment of reunion.

Soul retrieval work is important, necessary work. But it isn't always beautiful.

This was different. This was a beautiful return of something I never truly lost, only forgot.

The Elements and Spirit Allies

The elements that most people recognize are Earth, Air, Fire, and Water. There's a fifth that's often overlooked: Ether. Ether represents the energetic or spiritual realm, the space in which everything else exists.

Each element carries qualities. Fire burns, but it also renews. Water can destroy, but it purifies and sustains life. Air clears, moves, and brings change. Earth grounds, stabilizes, and nourishes. Most elements hold both creation and destruction within them, just as they do in the natural world.

There's a reason we intuitively associate certain meanings with them. Energetically, they embody those same principles.

I also understand that the lower chakras correspond to these elements. They exist in our bodies, in nature, and in the energetic realm simultaneously. In that sense, the elements are not separate from us; they're expressions of the same force moving through different forms.

At the broadest level, the elements are manifestations of divinity. They are ways consciousness expresses itself in forms we can recognize and work with. So when someone feels called to Fire, or Water, or Earth in a healing practice, what they're really responding to is an aspect of divinity that they need in that moment.

If you need warmth, renewal, or transformation, Fire may be what you're drawn to. If you need cleansing or emotional flow, Water is what you need. Grounding and safety might come through Earth. Clarity or movement through Air.

In practice, calling in an element is essentially calling in a specific quality of the Divine. From a narrower shamanic perspective, the elements also function symbolically and energetically. Fire burns away what no longer serves. Water cleanses and restores. Earth stabilizes. Air moves stagnant energy. Even without framing them spiritually, these forces work in predictable, embodied ways.

Spirit allies operate similarly. They are not separate from divinity; they are forms divinity takes so the human mind can receive it. People often encounter allies as ancestors, animals, guides, or religious figures. I've worked with people whose helping Spirit appeared as a deceased parent, a grandparent, or a close friend who had passed. That doesn't mean those beings *are* the source; it means that's the form the source takes so the person can understand and integrate what's being offered.

Our minds are limited. Our nervous systems are limited. Pure, undifferentiated consciousness would be overwhelming. Divinity meets us where we are.

If a person's father showed up as a helping Spirit, it's often because of the qualities associated with that relationship: protection, wisdom, compassion, strength, and guidance. Those qualities are what's being transmitted.

For me, one of my allies appears as Jesus. Not because I believe divinity is limited to that form, but because my mind understands compassion, healing, rebellion against injustice, and love through that image. That's the language my consciousness speaks.

If divinity showed up as a blinding light with no form, I wouldn't be able to assimilate it. Most of us wouldn't. We need something recognizable, something relational. That's what allies are. They are not separate beings granting power. They are mirrors, showing us the qualities, lessons, and strengths already available to us, but filtered in a way we can receive.

Ultimately, elements and allies serve the same purpose: They make the infinite accessible. They help translate something vast into something human.

Guides, Discernment, and the Role of the Healer

It's important to distinguish the term "guides" from "energies."

From a teaching perspective, my teachers are very clear that we do not "work with guides" in the way that term is often used. *Guide* is a very broad label. Some guides may be benevolent, some are simply energies that see an open channel and speak through it.

That's very different from what I work with, which I was taught to refer to as "a teaching Spirit in human form" or "my council." The difference is agency.

In the shamanic realms, I am not being guided. I am collaborating. I'm in the body, which means I'm the one holding the reins. I decide what happens, what doesn't, and how the work unfolds. I'm not surrendering control, I'm exercising discernment.

That doesn't mean other practitioners are wrong if or when they use the term "guides." It just means the way information is accessed differs. For example, a psychic or medical intuitive often receives information in a waking or lightly altered brainwave state. They're open, receptive, and receiving impressions, images, sensations, and knowledge. It's a more passive process.

Shamanic journeying is different. It's an altered state, similar to but not the same brain wave state as deep meditation, where the practitioner is actively participating. You're moving through non-ordinary reality. You're engaging, asking questions, traveling, and interacting. You're not just open; you're intentional.

Neither approach is better or worse. They're simply different.

Where it becomes critical, at least in my experience is discernment. If someone doesn't understand the difference between their own energy and someone else's, if they don't understand spiritual hygiene, if they don't know how to set boundaries or say no, or if they haven't done their own healing work, then they are essentially shining a spotlight on themselves energetically and opening the door to *anything* coming through. At that point, they're more of a channel than a director.

In shamanic work, I see myself as a director. I'm not channeling external entities. I'm working through my highest self, with support from my council (representations of divinity), but I remain responsible for the choices made during the work.

That responsibility carries weight.

Whether you're a psychic, a shaman, a witch, or anything else, discernment is everything. It affects accuracy, safety, and integrity. Discernment only develops through experience and practice. Natural ability helps, but it's not enough on its own.

The question came up: Does your council (guides) change depending on the person you're working with? Are they coming into the journey for you or for the client?

I have my council, and they remain consistent. Within that council, there are specific ones who've identified their roles; some assist with soul retrieval, others with different forms of healing. When I'm doing specific work, I call on the ones best suited for that purpose. Over time, through daily practice and journeying, I've built relationships with them. I know their strengths. I know how they support the work.

When I work with someone else, I ask my council to communicate with that person's guides. I don't usually interact directly with their guides unless that's explicitly part of the work. It's more like my council working with theirs. That keeps boundaries clean.

I don't send my council out casually or without intention. But if there's a situation, someone I know personally, or a large collective event like a tragedy, I can ask for support to be offered, always with respect and restraint.

Most of the time, I stay in my own wheelhouse. I work with the relationships I've built, the trust that's been established. I avoid inserting myself into someone else's energetic space unnecessarily. It's part of maintaining an ethical practice.

Healing Beyond the Self: Lineage, Land, and Collective Care

In shamanic work, healing often extends beyond the individual to ancestors, lineage, and collective wounds. It's an important part of our training. During my formal training, we did some form of collective healing work at least once a month, and we're encouraged to practice it individually as well. We've seen remarkable outcomes, but the purpose is never to *control* the outcome.

For example, there was someone struggling to get approval for a service dog. As a group, we asked permission to include them in a collective practice. They agreed. We sent supportive energy through our guides, without attachment or expectation. Later, the person came back and said, "I don't know what you did, but everything suddenly came together. The issue resolved itself."

Sometimes it's immediate. Sometimes it isn't.

There was another situation involving a plane crash. In that case, the intention wasn't to *fix* anything. We understood we might never see or know the impact. The practice was simply to send support, love, steadiness, and presence to the families and communities affected.

That's an important distinction. We're not interfering with karma. We're not directing outcomes. We're offering support and trusting that something larger than us knows how to use it. Collective energy is powerful, and you have to be careful with it.

Take something like drought. It's easy to say, "I'm going to pray for rain." But if rain comes too fast or too heavy, you create flooding and destruction. Instead of asking for a specific outcome, I journey and ask: *How can this be supported without causing harm?* What comes through isn't "more rain," but encouraging the roots of plants to grow deeper, so they can pull moisture upward, cool the soil, and restore balance. That creates conditions where rain can come sustainably.

It's not about manifesting a result. It's about supporting balance.

This brings up the subject of doing "healing work" on behalf of others. When it comes to other people, I have very firm boundaries. I never do any healing work for people who haven't asked for it.

The information that comes through intuitively can be highly sensitive. No one knows where someone else is in their healing process. Doing any type of shamanic work I do, without being asked to, would be a violation of my ethics and their privacy. I've had that done to me. It's unsettling. It creates fear, not safety.

Earth is different, but even there, I'm careful. I mostly focus on land that's within my stewardship—our property and our woods. That's where I have responsibility and consent.

For years, I received messages about placing my medicine wheel where it is now. I didn't act on it until I trusted those messages. Since then, the land has been healing alongside me. When we started restoring the woods, I expected grief from the plants, animals, and soil, but what I felt was relief. Like the land was saying, "Thank you for paying attention."

When I travel, I feel the energy of places very strongly. Alaska, for example, felt like it wanted to wrap me in a hug.

If I feel called to offer support, I'll sit on the ground, place my hands on the earth, and send energy into the land with love and intention. I do this quietly, without spectacle. Sometimes I'll touch a tree, grass, or stone. It's something I try to do wherever I go.

This is reciprocal; the land gives back as much as it receives.

Note that if something is full, it can't receive. If you're empty, you can't give. That's why, in every prayer or energy practice, if I'm asking for something to be removed—pain, illness, imbalance—I consciously replace it with something else. Healing, peace, strength.

The same applies to the Earth. If I'm offering energy, I also receive it. Time on the land replenishes me. That reciprocity is part of the healing—for the Earth and for us.

A Conversation: Balancing Your Own Healing While Guiding Others

Gina: How do you balance your own healing journey while being a guide, or a witness, for other people?

Heather: It is crucial to note that I can't help heal parts in someone else that I haven't faced in myself. That's rule number one. If I haven't healed it, or at least done my honest work around it, then I'm not the right person for that work.

Another important side to this work is that my motivation was never, "I'm doing this to heal myself." I have a reminder in my bathroom that says, *Remember why you started.* I started because I felt called into devotion, into a spiritual path, not because I was hunting healing as the goal.

Gina: When you say "healing," are you talking physical and emotional or soul-level?

Heather: All of it!

I've never gone into my practice thinking, *This is going to fix me.* I don't meditate as a self-improvement strategy. I don't pray with the goal of getting something from God. My driving force is devotion.

There are practices that have direct healing effects that can be used to move energy toward parts of the body that are hurt. I didn't even know that when I began learning about energy work. And I still don't practice *for* that result.

Healing is a byproduct. Devotion is the point.

Gina: And how does that connect to balance? To be a guide for others while still being human?

Heather: Here's the practical part. When you do healing work, you move a tremendous amount of energy, more than I ever understood was happening at first. And my balance is, *I need an outlet for that movement.*

Until I started on this journey and doing this work, I never fully understood the term, "My cup runneth over." I thought it meant that when you have a lot, you should give a lot. What I've learned is that when your cup is full, you give the part that would've run over. More so, you can't give from an empty cup. The balance comes from keeping your cup full but also giving away or using what is surplus.

Because the channel is open, the energy is there. If I don't move it, it doesn't just "sit quietly." Meditation helps move a large amount of it, but even with my extensive meditative practices, I end up with a surplus. It can create real funkiness in my body. My body gets sick. I feel off. So the work on others becomes an avenue for that energy to move through instead of building up inside me.

In a strange way, I get as much out of doing the work as the other person does, just in a different way.

Gina: There's also the piece of giving, of being an instrument. We were talking about St. Francis the other day and the Peace Prayer we both love. Would you say this is a tool for living a life of "sacred surrender"?

Heather: Yes. That is one of my prayers every day: that I am an instrument for peace, love, kindness, and understanding. This way "Heather" doesn't get in the way. I'm not the doer. I'm the vessel. That's how I keep it clean.

Gina: You mentioned the "hits" you get about people you love and trust. You've had that forever. Long before Kriya, long before shamanic study. At least since I've known you. How has that changed?

Heather: It's stronger now, but yes, it was always there. And here's the caveat: This was my soul's path the whole time. What created the sickness wasn't the sensitivity; it was me trying to deny it. Trying to repress it. Trying to live like it wasn't real. I knew what was happening, but I didn't want to acknowledge it.

Surrendering to the gifts

I no longer deny my gifts.

Yes, I can read tarot.

Yes, I can help you connect with your power animal.

Yes, I can help you reconnect with lost parts.

Yes, I can see spirits and help them cross over/move on.

Yes, I can tell when a friend is in distress thousands of miles away.

Now, I've learned how to channel it all in a grounded, helpful way. How to take information and turn it into knowing and discernment.

It was always there. I just didn't always let it be what it was.

Combining the remembering with my other spiritual practices and study, I now know that remembering can be a trap in and of itself. If I remember it, then I've experienced it before, and that makes reconnecting with it a pattern. While I love what Shamanism has given me, I don't see myself hanging a "permanent shingle" on my door and charging for my services in a traditional way.

You might be asking, "Why not?"

If you remember what I reiterated a few paragraphs ago, I talked about remembering why I started. I didn't start on this path to become a shaman. I started on this path because I wanted to devote my life to my higher power, to find out who I really am, and to heal my own trauma and connection to soul.

The gifts that I was born with and have developed along this path are gifts I'm grateful to have. But in order to go deeper, to connect deeper, I have to acknowledge that the gifts are also a distraction. If you remember, I said, "Patterns repeat so that we have opportunities to heal, to grow, and to change our karma." If this pattern is repeating, it is just as much the same pattern as the painful parts.

Does that mean I won't help others using shamanic practices as I move forward on the path? No. Does that mean that my soul's path isn't as a soul healer? Also, no.

It means that I can take what I've learned and continue to learn, apply it in new ways, and follow new patterns. Patterns that won't distract me from my course—my course of devotion and continued spiritual growth.

CHAPTER FOURTEEN

Remembering, Integration, and Practical Practice

What Humanity is Being Asked to Remember

I wholeheartedly believe we're being invited to remember, and in the remembering, there's an unbecoming.

An unbecoming of everything that isn't real.

Yes, there's awakening—the idea that we're divine beings and consciousness is bigger than what we've been taught. But this was always true, always there. We're just remembering now.

Forgiveness, compassion, and love all shift when you see pain as a collective pattern instead of a personal failure.

When the glass is dark, when it's caked over, it's like being in a cave. It's hard to remember there's light on the other side. When you're in that cave, it becomes all about you. That's all you can feel. That's all you can see.

But it is in forgiveness, especially forgiving yourself, where the first crack is created for light to come in. Forgiving your soul for choosing this life. This path. These lessons. These people. This pain. When that crack of light comes through, you start to remember: *There's a whole world outside the cave.*

You realize you're a tiny point in something infinite.

Then the question becomes: *If I've felt this, how many others have felt this too? If I've found my way through, how can I be a light for someone else finding their way in?*

That's when we start moving from personal survival to collective care. The truth is, the changes we make are never only for us.

We could stay in our cocoon. We survived there. We'd survive there again. But when we change, it ripples. It touches our partners, our children, and our communities. It touches the Earth. Every small shift in the glass lets more light through, and collectively, our lights begin to shine brighter.

Our lives here are finite. The moment we're born, this incarnation is already moving toward its end. It's never just about us.

Integration and Everyday Sacredness

Integration is about understanding. Understanding that the "download" comes first and the meaning of it filters in later. Sometimes over days. Sometimes over years. In the beginning, I didn't understand this concept fully or the reason behind it.

You only receive what you can actually assimilate.

The way you create space for assimilation is the work: reflection, meditation, therapy, quieting the mind, shadow work, time in nature, and physical movement that allows you to release attachments and connect with Spirit. That's how the system clears. The meanings come through. The glass starts to clear.

As you learn how integration works, you stop fighting it. You recognize it. You let it settle. You ask better questions. You learn to apply it instead of resisting it.

In real life, integration might look like this: The difference between walking into a room and assuming everyone is judging you versus realizing that it's your mind pulling you back into old patterns. Or it might look like this: The difference between being triggered and reacting versus being able to step outside it and ask, *What's happening here? Why am I reacting this way? Is this who I want to be right now? How do I want to show up?*

Integration isn't always flashy. It's life-changing, but it shows up in small moments. You still feel emotions. I still get angry. I still get sad. But it passes quicker. It's fleeting. And if it doesn't pass, if someone keeps picking at the scab, then there's still something to learn there.

What brings me back? Practice. My daily practice.

It is in the work that we assimilate. It is in the practice that we absorb. And it is in the deep work and the practice together that we clear the glass to let the light through.

To this day, I prioritize the practice. I meditate at least twice a day. Even if it's only fifteen minutes. It's a recalibration. A remembering. I still go to therapy. I still do bodywork. I still see my own shaman. I still go to my Western doctor.

I'm still Heather in a human body.

My daily practice reminds me that I'm part of something much bigger. I'm just a tiny part of it all, and that's okay. It's more than okay; it's the whole point. It's why devotion is such an important part of this journey.

Your practice doesn't have to look the same every day. When I'm with friends, I might not do the full practice I do when I'm alone. But the devotion stays. The return stays.

Scientifically, we know meditation brings the brain back to a calmer baseline. It's not just spiritual; it's physiological. It's an actual prescription.

Making the Practice Real for Real People

You've made it far, and you might be saying, "Geez, Heather, that's great, but I don't have four hours a day."

Trust that I get it. I know what it is like to have a full-time job, a part-time job, two young kids, and a house to take care of. Your life is full of responsibilities, and no doubt you have some giant to-do list. Work, business, kids, a partner, school, aging parents, pets, a house, and a car, and life keeps moving at warp speed.

That is precisely why taking time to connect with your soul and with "that something bigger" is so important. There will come a time that you want that clouded glass cleaner. Why not start now?

As I mentioned earlier, as little as fifteen minutes. Just fifteen minutes in the morning and fifteen minutes at night for your practice of choice is enough to make a world of difference.

Most people spend longer than that scrolling on their phones. Even with kids, with a job, with all the responsibilities, you can carve out thirty minutes. Of course, you have to want to. You have to crave that healing, that connection, that level of pure love that only the Divine gives you.

What you focus on grows.

If you say your job is more important, it will be.

If you think time scrolling is more important, it will be.

If you believe your family is more important, it will be. There is zero judgement here; it is just the way it is—a simple fact.

But, if you don't make time for your inner life, your inner connection, and your healing, in the end, you, your family, and your responsibilities will all suffer.

How do I know? It happened to me.

Ignoring the inner calling, ignoring the healing my soul needed, and letting my body take the brunt of it all led to not just my suffering. My business crumbled, and my husband and my grown children were all put through tremendous stress.

I'm not expecting anyone to live like I live. My kids are grown. I'm not in the thick of parenting. I'm at a stage of life where I can choose this, so I do. My focus is faith. Devotion. Becoming the highest version of myself. We are all in different stages of our journey. There is no specific time requirement for any practice you choose. Goodness, there isn't even a right or wrong way to do anything you chose to do to connect to higher self.

This book is for you:

You, who feels called.

You, who craves a deeper, purer kind of love.

You, who knows there is more to this whole crazy thing we call life than the day-to-day.

Let me be just one example for you; I'm the poster child for "it's not one-size-fits-all."

Meditation works for me now, but I know it's not applicable to everyone in the same way. And not all meditation is the same. I studied Buddhist meditation for two years. At the time, it didn't click for me. For whatever the reason was: my kids were young, my body was terribly uncomfortable sitting still for that long, and more importantly, spiritually, it didn't click for me then.

The invitation is: Find what resonates. Find the practice you feel called to. Find the practice you will actually do consistently. Ideally once a day, more if you can. You are not looking for perfection, but connection. Consistency is more important than the time you practice daily. Give yourself grace. Nobody starts at 2–4 hours a day of anything. You build.

My message in almost everything is: Give yourself some grace. Listen to what your soul tells you it needs. Most of the time, the hardest part is sitting long enough to hear it. Your soul knows what it needs, which means it knows what *you* need. You just have to give it room to speak.

A Reminder That You Were Never Broken

You've never been broken. Your soul has been around since the beginning of time. Our intuition is our soul talking to us. That soul has been here a long time; we've just gotten really good at shutting it out. It starts when we're young. The soul says: *Caution.* Or: *Move forward.* Or: *Wait.* And we don't listen. That's what's "broken," not the soul. Not who you are. But the part that says that you *shouldn't* listen. Think about it: Would ignoring something that ancient, that wise, and that steady make sense? It doesn't.

It's as if the Universe itself came to you to talk, to tell you something, and you ignored it.

You're not broken. Your mind is telling you that you are. Your ego self has gotten in the way. Society has gotten in the way. You've lived in a world that praises doing, not being. And the accumulation of trauma has clouded the glass.

My friend, it is time to clear the glass. It's time to let the light shine through. It's time to give yourself the gift of reconnecting with your Divine Self. You started a journey. Whether it's a healing journey, a spiritual journey, a reconnection journey, or just a curiosity journey—you are here.

Right now, I want you to put one hand on your heart. No rush, the book will be right here waiting for you.

Put one hand on your heart.

Take a long, slow deep breath in.

Then let it back out just as slowly.

Now take another.

Remember why you started.

Remember who you are.

Take another breath.

Hold true to those two things: why you started and who you are. Make them your focus. When you keep those in view, the rest falls into place.

Your brain will lie to you. Your body will try to listen to your brain—until it can't. Life and the outside world will try to derail you.

Those two things will keep you steady on your path: Remember why you started. Remember who you are.

Why did I start?

To experience creation. To be a living expression of the Divine.

And who am I?

Infinite.

From one soul to another: *remember why you started, and remember who you are.*

CHAPTER FIFTEEN

Togetherness, Forgiveness, and Remembering

We Are Not Alone

At some point on a healing path, something subtle changes.

You begin to notice that when you speak honestly about what you've lived through, people lean in. Not out of curiosity, out of recognition. Something in your story mirrors something in them. This realization emerges slowly, through conversation, through practice, or through the simple act of doing the work.

As I moved deeper into shamanic training and began working with others, I noticed that the very things that helped me survive spiritually, emotionally, and physically were helping others too.

When I work with people, I'm not reliving my past or projecting my experiences onto theirs. In shamanic terms, I become what's known as a *hollow bone*: a vessel through which healing moves. My focus shifts to her, him, or them receiving the healing. My job is to listen, translate, filter, and offer what can be received without harm.

Healing isn't about revealing everything. It's about telling a story that heals rather than retraumatizes. It's about knowing when silence is kinder than truth, and when truth must be delivered gently enough to land.

And still, even for healers, we are not immune to being human.

There are moments when someone else's story breaks through the protections. When parallels appear. When old wounds stir. That's when even shamans need shamans. That's when the reminder becomes clear again: You are not meant to do this alone.

No matter where you are in your journey, whether you are just beginning, deep in your journey, or quietly supporting others, you are part of a larger web of remembering. Every person you meet, every conversation you have, every kindness or cruelty carries weight.

You are not invisible in this process.

You are not alone.

The Call to Remember

At its core, this invitation is simple.

We are being asked to remember who we really are.

Not our job titles.

Not our relationships.

Not our roles, achievements, failures, or identities assigned by culture or circumstance.

But who we are beneath all of that.

Who *you* really are: pure love and light.

As cliché as it sounds, you are infinite. Underneath your humanity, you are pure infinite love. Each soul arrives with its own purpose, its own curriculum, and its own reason for being here, and none of it can be measured by external markers.

On a collective level, humanity is in the midst of remembering this truth again. History moves in cycles. Awareness rises, falls, and rises again. We are currently on an upward curve, and remembering is contagious.

Every time one person chooses compassion over bitterness, presence over distraction, or love over fear, it ripples outward. You teach without meaning to. You influence without knowing it. You become part of someone else's story simply by how you show up.

The Tale Of Two Wolves

One evening, an elderly Cherokee Brave told his grandson about a battle that goes on inside people.

He said, "My son, the battle is between two 'wolves' inside us all. One is evil. It is anger, envy, jealousy, sorrow, regret, greed, arrogance, self-pity, guilt, resentment, inferiority, lies, false pride, superiority, and ego. The other is good. It is joy, peace, love, hope, serenity, humility, kindness, benevolence, empathy, generosity, truth, compassion, and faith."

The grandson thought about it for a minute and then asked his grandfather, "Which wolf wins?"

The grandfather replied, "The one you feed."

— Quote found on the Nanticoke Indian Tribe website

Collective healing happens one interaction at a time. The moment you begin treating yourself with the same compassion you extend to others, something profound changes. The capacity to love widens. Grace becomes available. Forgiveness—real forgiveness—becomes possible.

Remembering Without Bypassing

Remembering does not mean skipping pain.

Healing cannot happen merely by thinking positively. It cannot be mindfully meditated away, yoga-ed away, or spiritualized out of the body. Those practices can support healing, but they cannot replace it.

Emotions were given to us as tools, signals meant to protect and inform us. Anger isn't wrong. Fear isn't bad. Grief isn't failure. The problem begins when emotions take up permanent residence, replaying old wounds that never had the chance to heal.

When a reaction feels disproportionate, it usually is, not because the feeling is invalid, but because it carries more than the present moment. It holds the weight of everything that came before it.

Healing begins by acknowledging what's there without judgment. Asking where it came from. Listening long enough to understand what it's asking for. And it's just as important to know when to rest. There is wisdom in pausing. In stepping away from analysis. In reading a novel instead of another self-help book. In walking outside. Letting things settle is key to integrating what we learn. Most of the time integration happens in stillness, not effort.

Support is essential, especially when the pain runs deep. When it lives in the body, the psyche, or the soul, you must invite and receive support. Therapy, medical care, spiritual guidance—these work together to help you do the work and clear the glass.

Healing works best when it's allowed to be whole.

Forgiveness Returns Us to Wholeness

Forgiveness is often misunderstood.

It is not excusing harm.

It is not erasing accountability.

It is not a moral obligation placed on those who were wounded.

At its deepest level, forgiveness begins inward.

If the soul chooses experiences for growth, not as punishment but as curriculum, the first forgiveness required is toward oneself. Toward the self that lived it. Toward the self that survived it. Toward the soul that chose to walk this path at all. Until compassion exists for the self, forgiveness for others remains surface-level.

This isn't about forgiving perpetrators before you're ready. It's about releasing the belief that you were broken for having lived what you lived.

When that belief loosens, anger softens. Resentment loses its grip. The trauma no longer defines who you are.

Deep healing starts with compassion for oneself and learning to embrace forgiveness. Healing, remembering, and purpose will follow. Your deep work matters more than you know. The more deeply you heal yourself, the more healing becomes possible everywhere else.

Living the Sacred in Ordinary Life

Sacredness does not require retreats, robes, or hours of uninterrupted silence. It lives in the kitchen sink, in the email replies, in grocery store lines, in traffic, and in how you eat, breath, and speak.

While my devotion may look disciplined with daily intentional practices, the invitation is not to follow my steps. Your invitation is to find reverence where you already are.

Eating is a practice; food carries energy. Drinking water is a practice; water carries memory. Stepping outside is a practice; nature carries existence. Bodies respond to intention. Gratitude changes chemistry. Presence changes digestion. None of this is mystical; it's physiological.

Sacred living begins with attention. Attention to intention. Sacredness is all around us. It's in the air we breathe. It's in the soil you walk on. It lives in the plants, the animals, and most importantly, it lives in you.

When life becomes messy, and it will, devotion becomes an anchor. It offers refuge from the chaos. When the noise quiets, clarity returns.

Devotion evolves. It matures.

What begins as belief becomes practice. What begins as curiosity becomes embodiment. When you embrace the sacredness around and within, you become the truest expression of who you've always been.

Ordinary Lives, Divine Moments

Many people are taught they are "just" something.

Just a housewife.

Just a worker.

Just ordinary.

Divinity does not belong to titles. It appears in moments of surrender, like choosing play over getting frustrated when caught in a rainstorm with your children. Or releasing possessions that no longer serve you. Like noticing autumn leaves while driving and offering quiet gratitude for their beauty.

Sacred moments don't announce themselves. They reveal themselves when we are present enough to notice.

When survival takes over, the body knows first: muscles tighten, breath shortens, and thoughts harden. These signals are invitations asking for pause, breath, grounding, nature, and touch.

Returning to sacredness only requires awareness.

The Offering

If I could whisper just one truth into your ear, it would be this: *Who you really are is enough.*

This book is not meant to convince, convert, or instruct. It is an offering—a reminder that another way exists, that connection is possible, and that isolation is not the truth of your life.

The hope planted here is simple:

That you feel less alone.

That you feel seen.

That you remember something you've always known lives inside you.

To carry you forward, I leave you with love and one of my favorite prayers:

O Lord, make me an instrument of thy peace.

Where there is hatred, let me bring love;

Where there is resentment, let me bring forgiveness;

Where there is discord, let me bring unity;

Where there is doubt, let me bring faith;

Where there is error, let me bring truth;

Where there is despair, let me bring happiness;

Where there is sadness, let me bring joy;

Where there is darkness, let me bring light.

O Master, grant that I may desire rather

To console than to be consoled,

To understand rather than to be understood,

To love rather than to be loved,

Because it is in giving, that we receive,

In forgiving, that we obtain forgiveness,

In dying, that we rise to eternal life.

~Saint Francis of Assissi

That is the invitation. And it is open.

CHAPTER SIXTEEN

Where The Ordinary Soul Healer Comes Full Circle

This book began at a moment of rupture—a retreat, a silence, a summons that made itself impossible to ignore. At the time, it felt like a calling outward to heal, to guide, and to serve.

What revealed itself slowly, and then all at once, was something far more humbling.

A soul healer is not someone who heals or "fixes" others. A soul healer is someone willing to heal themselves deeply enough that their presence becomes an invitation rather than an instruction.

Every soul is tasked with healing its own experience in this life. Some do so quietly. Some publicly. Some through ceremony, others through parenting, partnership, grief, or endurance. No path is higher than another.

The extraordinary does not belong to mystics alone. It lives all around us, in ordinary houses, aging bodies, changing seasons, and quiet acts of courage.

What makes this journey I am on feel extraordinary is not uniqueness, but timing. This is simply the lifetime in which remembrance arrived for me.

This book is part of my extraordinary journey toward healing and living a more sacred life, day by day. What started as a calling during a twenty-one-day retreat in the summer of 2025 also came full circle during a silent retreat in the winter of 2026 in that same Ashram. The message was clear: *We are all soul healers.*

You, too, are a soul healer. Soul healer isn't a title, or a vocation; it is a gift. A gift we all have access to. When you work to heal yourself, you contribute to the healing of the collective.

Light does not need to be announced. It only needs to be lived.

Wherever you find yourself on this journey, you're exactly where you're meant to be. And always remember, who you really are has always been enough.

If anything has been offered here, let it be this: You, too, are a soul healer. May light shine through your glass.

With love and Humility,

~ Heather Debreceni

Afterword

BY GINA STENBACK

Sacredness Has Never Required a Stage

When Heather first asked me to help her write this book, I didn't fully understand what I was stepping into. I knew it would be deep. Heather is not one to do anything halfway. And anyone who knows us knows we don't do small talk, and we don't take real conversations lightly.

I thought I was signing up to help bring her story to life through interviews, transcripts, shaping narrative, and refining language. What I didn't know was—how sacred the process would be.

From the first recording, it became clear this wasn't just a memoir. It wasn't simply the story of a woman healing from trauma, navigating faith, or returning to devotion. It was something more intimate: a reclamation of soul.

For her—and, in many ways, for me too.

Reclamation is not tidy work. It requires honesty, surrender, and a willingness to feel what has long been held beneath the surface.

There were days after our recordings when I would sit quietly, staring at the screen long after our call had ended. Not because I didn't know what to write, but because I felt it. The truth of it. The recognition of it.

You cannot sit with someone in their journey to *remembering* without confronting your own. That was the part I didn't anticipate.

I've known Heather for years. I've watched her move through careers, locations, illness, doubt, faith, collapse, and rebuilding. But sitting with her through these intense conversations, hearing her speak not as a role, but as truest self something deep shifted. For her. For me. For both of us.

There is something powerful about watching someone stop apologizing for who they are. Not in a sudden or loud way, simply with intention, commitment and conviction.

Heather has always been a deeply spiritual being. You can sense that the minute you step close to her presence. What changed was her willingness to be seen that way, without flinching. Her willingness to say, "This is who I am," without asking for permission.

And in witnessing that, I had to ask myself:

Where am I still shrinking?

Where am I still performing?

Where am I still editing my truth before it leaves my mouth?

Books don't just transform readers. They transform the people who help bring them into the world.

There were moments of lightness, unexpected interruptions, shared laughter, and ordinary moments unfolding along the deeper conversations. Conversations around trauma, faith, forgiveness, love, and God. These moments, though unexpected, were so grounding.

And that's the point: *Sacredness has never required a stage.*

It shows up in kitchens, in quiet mornings, in difficult conversations, and in the small, unnoticed choices we make every day. That sacredness showed up in this process again and again.

One of the clearest realizations for me was this: The extraordinary rarely looks extraordinary while it's happening. It hides in the ordinary.

In the woman cleaning her home.

In the parent showing up when it's hard.

In the quiet devotion that no one else sees.

The title of this book is not ironic. It is precise. There is something powerful about recognizing that an "ordinary" life can hold extraordinary depth, devotion, and truth. And it holds those without needing to become anything else.

We are taught that spiritual authority requires visibility, titles, and perfection. It doesn't. It requires devotion. And if there's one thing I've learned while writing this book, it is that devotion is available to anyone.

Throughout this process, I watched Heather move from explaining her path to standing in it, being with it, and doing it with conviction.

Certainty does not need to convince. It simply exists. Watching her stand in that certainty changed something in me. It invited me to look more honestly at my own life. The roles I've carried, the identities I've held, and where I've allowed them to define me more than they should.

At the heart of this book is a simple invitation: *Remember who you are.*

Not the roles.

Not the expectations.

Not the stories handed to you before you had language for them.

You are not broken.

You never were.

You may be layered. You may be wounded. You may be navigating patterns that were never yours to begin with.

But you are not broken.

In fact, it's the opposite; you're a perfect being of pure consciousness underneath it all.

Writing this book required both of us to sit with discomfort. To allow nuance. To speak with raw honesty, without simplifying, sensationalizing, or distorting.

What stayed with me most is this:

How many people are walking through life believing they are "just" something?

Just a mother.

Just a partner.

Just a job or title.

Just a role.

Just surviving.

And how many of them are carrying something far deeper within them?

If this book offers you anything, I hope it is this:

That when you close it, you feel less alone. Not because there are answers here, but because something in these pages reflects something in you.

I hope it gives you permission. Permission to look at your life more honestly, question what no longer fits, and recognize both the ordinary and the extraordinary within you.

I am not the same person who began this project. Witnessing someone return to themselves changes you. It makes you more raw with your honesty. More uninhibited in how you look at the world. More present. More willing to listen. More open to the moments that unfold in front of you.

Let it do the same for you.

Choose yourself in small ways. Forgive yourself, slowly and fully. Notice what has always been there and what no longer belongs. Transformation rarely looks dramatic, it happens through consistency and in the little daily things. And remember: *Who you are is already and has always been enough.*

Heather's story is hers.

But...

The invitation is yours.

If something in you stirs while reading this, it is not a coincidence.

It is remembering.

With love,
Gina

Acknowledgements

WITH GRATITUDE

This book has been brought to life through the love, support, and guidance of many, and it is with deep gratitude and humility that I offer my thanks.

First and foremost, I extend my heartfelt appreciation to Gina Stenback for the tremendous care, dedication, and presence she offered throughout this process. Her ability to hold a safe and compassionate space allowed my spoken words to be translated into written form with authenticity and grace. Without her steady support and willingness to meet me in vulnerability, this book would not have come together as it has.

I offer my sincere gratitude to Swami Atmavidyananda Giri and Swami Sahajananda, as well as to all the swamis, yogacharyas, and the greater Kriya Yoga community. Your presence, teachings, and support have been a guiding light along my spiritual path, and I am deeply grateful for the role each of you has played in my journey.

To the beta readers who so generously gave their time and thoughtful feedback, thank you for helping to shape this work into something that is both accessible and meaningful. Your insights were invaluable in ensuring that these words could be received as they were intended.

I am also deeply grateful to Carrie Sargent of The Final Punctuation for her careful attention and dedication in refining this manuscript. Her work brought clarity and polish to the final version, making it ready to be shared.

To Sima Harrison for her beautiful artwork and bringing my cover vision to life.

To the many healing arts practitioners who have supported me along the way—far too many to name individually—I offer my sincere thanks. Your time, energy, and care have been an integral part of my growth and healing.

To my mother, thank you for showing me, throughout my life, the true beauty of a mother's unconditional love.

To my sister, my first and lifelong friend, thank you for walking beside me from my very first breath

To my children, thank you for teaching me, in countless ways, how to be a better human being.

And to my husband, thank you for your patience, your steady presence, and your unwavering support throughout this entire journey.

To each of you, I offer my deepest gratitude.

With love and humility,

Heather

About the author

HEATHER DEBRECENI

Heather Debreceni is a spiritual mentor, shamanic practitioner, devoted yogi, ordained reverend, speaker, and author whose work lives at the intersection of trauma, healing, chronic health patterns, identity, and spiritual awakening.

Her path has not been simple. Through her own lived experience with pain, illness, loss, and deep personal transformation, Heather came to understand that healing is not about becoming someone new. It is about returning to the truth of who we already are. Her work is grounded in that understanding — helping others reconnect with their bodies, their inner wisdom, their lives, and something greater than themselves.

Heather's approach is honest, compassionate, and deeply human. She does not separate the physical from the spiritual, nor does she believe there is only one "right" way to heal. Through mentorship, speaking, and group experiences, she offers a grounded path back to clarity, wholeness, and the sacred self.

To learn more about Heather's work visit https://heatherdebreceni.com/

166 HEATHER DEBRECENI

To learn more about Heather's work visit https://heatherdebreceni.com/